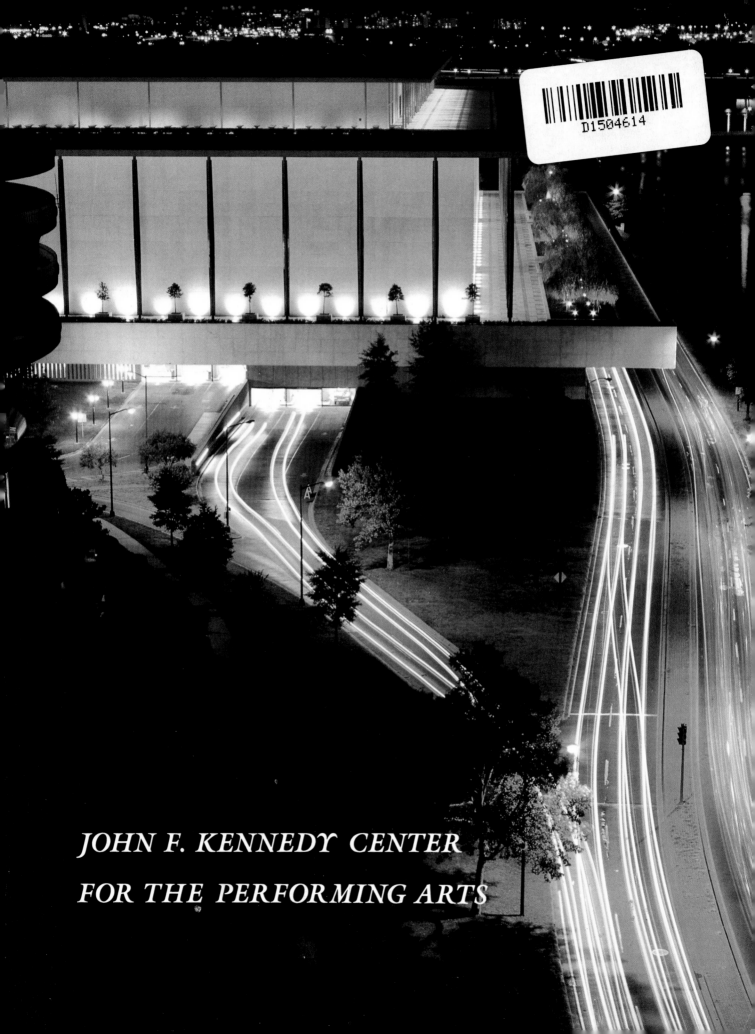

JOHN F. KENNEDY CENTER
FOR THE PERFORMING ARTS

I AM CERTAIN THAT AFTER
THE DUST OF CENTURIES
HAS PASSED OVER OUR CITIES,
WE, TOO, WILL BE REMEMBERED

NOT FOR OUR VICTORIES OR DEFEATS
IN BATTLE OR IN POLITICS,
BUT FOR OUR CONTRIBUTION
TO THE HUMAN SPIRIT

JOHN FITZGERALD KENNEDY

Designed by Philip Grushkin

John F. Kennedy Center
for the Performing Arts

BRENDAN GILL

HARRY N. ABRAMS, INC., Publishers, New York

The text on pages 17-52 appeared originally in *The New Yorker*.

Library of Congress Catalog Card Number: 81-69638
International Standard Book Number: 0-8109-1206-6 (cloth), 0-8109-2263-0 (paper)

Printed and bound in the United States.

CONTENTS

The Grand Foyer is one of the largest rooms in the world. Here an audience is filling it for a concert during a Mozart festival in 1974.

Many a Broadway hit has been launched from beneath the benign roof of the Kennedy Center. Not the least among them is "42nd Street," which has been one of the most popular musical comedies in New York City during the 1980–1981 season and may well run forever.

The corps of the American Ballet Theatre, the Center's official company, in Mikhail Baryshnikov's "The Nutcracker," which had its world premiere at the Kennedy Center in 1976.

ACKNOWLEDGMENTS

IN THE PREPARATION of books of this nature, thanks must flow outward as the sparks fly upward. A large number of people have put their time, talent, and energy at my disposal, and I salute them all. Not least among them is Yoichi Okamoto, who has a gift for taking pictures that are both of this world and out of it. An unusually well-grounded technique leads to consequences unexpectedly poetic; his eye and that of his camera teach us to perceive more than what we merely see. Other photographs are by Fletcher Drake, Richard Braaten, and Jack Buxbaum; my gratitude to them. Jack Buxbaum is to be especially commended for the detective skills he practiced in ransacking the Center's files and locating again and again the very picture we needed. Let me thank as well the staff of the Center's delightful Performing Arts Library, where Peter Fay and Cynthia Barkley provided me with amusement along with instruction. For their assistance in assembling the chronology, I thank Maria Pessoa and Clytie Salisbury, and for answering with alacrity and high spirits every vexatious question I put to them, my compliments to Geraldine Otremba of the Center, and Richard Sacks of *The New Yorker*. For having urged me to undertake the task, I bow to Jillian Poole, who, it appears, has yet to hear uttered in her presence the word "No."

B.G.

CORPORATIONS AND COUNTRIES are measured by the health and prosperity of people, by the opportunities people have to participate, to contribute, to grow, and by the freedom they have to make choices and build better lives for themselves, their children, and the children of their children.

Perhaps we think first of good jobs, equal rights, and fair rewards, but no less important are the measures of mind and heart and spirit: the prosperity of literature, art, music, and theatre, the culture of a community and a nation, and the appreciation of our past and anticipation of our future.

It is in this context that the International Paper Company and its Foundation support education and the arts where IP people work and live. Joyfully, we mark the first ten years of the Kennedy Center by making possible this celebration in print.

Edwin A. Gee
Chairman and Chief Executive Officer
International Paper Company

WELCOMING THE MUSES

THE JOHN F. KENNEDY CENTER FOR THE PERFORMING ARTS opened in Washington, D.C., on September 8, 1971. It was an opening that culminated thirteen years of strenuous preparation, with many difficulties overcome and much heartbreak endured, and it was the hope of everyone concerned that the occasion would prove of lasting historical significance. Looking back, we are able to measure how amply this hope has been realized. In the comparatively short period of a single decade, the Kennedy Center has become indispensable to Washington and, increasingly, to the country as a whole.

Today, the Center has begun to occupy the place in the cultural life of the United States that President Kennedy confidently predicted for it in October, 1963, when, a few weeks before his death, he gave a luncheon at the White House for a gathering of prominent businessmen. He was seeking to enlist their help in the construction of what was then known as the National Cultural Center; newspaper accounts of the luncheon describe the President as being "a persuasive salesman…pushing the Center with the fervor of a man sold on his own product." Kennedy assured his guests that the Center would belong equally to all Americans and that the need for it was dire. "The nations of the world," he said, "have their great and beautiful centers for the performing arts, but here in the world's greatest capital we have nothing."

A shocking statement, as the fervent salesman-President intended it to be; for it came close to summing up the truth about the condition of the performing arts in Washington in the early nineteen-sixties. The accommodations available for those arts were scant indeed; they consisted of one commercially operated legitimate theatre, one large hall that was not particularly well-suited to music, and a number of small auditoriums situated in museums, libraries, churches, and the like. Setting out on tour, some of the world's leading opera companies, symphony orchestras, and dance companies hesitated to include Washington on

Though an intimate auditorium had always been planned for the Center, the Terrace Theater, tucked above the Eisenhower Theater, did not reach the construction stage until the late seventies, when the government and people of Japan made a gift to the Center in honor of the Bicentennial of the United States. Roger L. Stevens, Chairman of the Center, checks on the progress being made.

Two sketches of the Center as it was originally designed by the architect Edward Durell Stone. For reasons of economy and efficiency, his water-lily-like pavilion, seeming to float along the sedgy bank of the Potomac River, gave way to the present, contentedly earthbound rectangular box. Luckily, the hanging planters never got past the drawing stage.

their itineraries; they were likely to encounter too many disadvantages in regard to seating capacity, box-office revenue, stage size, and backstage facilities. By the circular reasoning often observed at the point where the arts and business meet, the lack of theatres in Washington gave it the reputation of being an unprofitable theatre town, which led in turn to the opinion that it would be risky to build new theatres there. Most of the hundred or so countries that maintained embassies in Washington in those days were said to consider it a hardship post, thanks to its meagre cultural resources; if it was a matter of the graphic or glyptic arts, one could visit with pleasure such institutions as the National Gallery, the Corcoran Gallery, and the Phillips Collection, but in other respects Washington amounted to a near-wasteland.

This unfortunate state of affairs was ironic, because it was in Washington, more than in any other city in the country, that the Muses might have been expected to be made welcome. After all, it was a city brought into existence not by mere money-grubbing trade and manufacture but for a single mighty purpose: to be the seat of the federal government. It was the first city in history to have been created solely for the purpose of governance. For years, members of Congress had hotly debated the question of a permanent home for themselves and for those departments—the Treasury, the Patent Office, and so on—that even the sketchiest of central governments would feel obliged to establish. Congress had met in several places, including Philadelphia, which toward the end of the eighteenth century was the largest and most agreeably cosmopolitan of American cities, but there were reasons (having more to do with politics than with convenience) that a site somewhere further to the south was thought desirable. In 1790, largely in order to put an end to congressional bickering, George Washington was charged with selecting a site for the newly designated federal district. Not much to anyone's surprise but to the disappointment of many, Washington chose a tract of land on the banks of the Potomac River, a few miles upstream from his beloved Mount Vernon.

The District of Columbia, embracing within its earliest boundaries a hundred square miles, was taken in part from Virginia and in part from Maryland. In the eighteen-forties, perhaps in disheartenment over its slow growth, the District gave up portions of its territory; today it embraces approximately sixty-nine square miles. At the time it was laid out, the land of the District consisted of gently rolling hills, some under cultivation and the rest heavily wooded, with a number of creeks and much swampy land along the Potomac. (The Kennedy Center stands in a section of Washington commonly referred to as Foggy Bottom; it bore the same nickname a hundred and eighty years ago.) Two port cities, Alexandria and Georgetown, flourished within sight of the new capital and gave it access by ship to the most important cities of the infant nation—Charleston, Baltimore, Philadelphia, New York, Newport, Salem, and Portsmouth—as well as to far-off London and the Continent. As George Washington and Thomas Jefferson first imagined it, the capital was to be small and compact; Jefferson wrote to Washington, suggesting that the plan be based on a sequence of squares, not unlike the squares in Philadelphia, and he appended a map that implied the laying out of what was scarcely more than a village.

All such modest intentions were soon forgotten, thanks to the ambitious dreams of a French engineer named Pierre L'Enfant, whom Washington commissioned, in 1791, to draw up plans for the capital. An importunate firebrand, L'Enfant had grown up in Paris and Versailles, where his father was employed at court as an artist and designer of tapestries; from his earliest youth, L'Enfant had admired the baroque architecture of Versailles and the beauty of its gardens, created by Le Nôtre. Coming to America, L'Enfant had fought in the Revolution and undergone with Washington the hardships of Valley Forge. In temperament, L'Enfant was at the opposite pole from Washington, and it is fascinating to speculate on their conversations concerning the new city. L'Enfant must have been exceptionally eloquent; he succeeded in spellbinding all the figures chiefly concerned with the building of the capital, and the more he talked the bigger the project became.

L'Enfant's calculations in regard to the future of the country and the kind of architecture it would require were as grandiose as those of Boullée and other so-called "visionary" architects at work in France at that period. Even today, L'Enfant's optimism has the power to take our breath away. He predicted, for example, that the United States, which then had a population of only a few million people, would someday have a population of half a billion people (about twice our present population); he also predicted that Washington would have a population of half a million people (a total not reached until the 1930s). In the light of such expectations, L'Enfant set about designing a city on a prodigious scale. Jefferson's toy gridiron was swallowed up, with Jefferson's consent, by a complex extravaganza of broad, interlocking thoroughfares and green open spaces. The thoroughfares sprang like spokes from the hubs of wheels at points where the terrain happened to possess certain natural advantages. The most important of the hubs was situated on the high bluff where the capitol would be built; another important hub was at a gentle rise set aside for the President's house. The Mall was projected as a major axis running from the capitol west to the Potomac; a minor axis would run southward from the President's house, and where it intersected at right angles with the major axis an imposing public monument would catch the eye. (This monument turned out to be the colossal obelisk

An accurately detailed model of the projected Center having been constructed, a series of unveilings of the model took place in the autumn of 1962. The first of them was in Newport, Rhode Island, where the Kennedys often spent weekends at the summer home of Mrs. Kennedy's mother, Mrs. Hugh Auchincloss. Among those present were a number of theatrical personalities, including Paul Newman and his wife, Joanne Woodward, looking understandably startled by a cameraman's flashbulb.

raised in honor of Washington; by bad luck, the soil proved unstable at the designated place and the monument had to be built a few hundred feet off-center.)

If it was sufficiently remarkable that an urban design of a sophistication as yet unknown to London or Paris could be thought suitable for the capital of a young and struggling nation, still more remarkable was the determination to erect it in a near-wilderness, with little skilled labor available and few building materials except wood within easy hauling distance. Many people assumed that the new city would never be realized, and there were always members of Congress eager to press for a return to some already well-established metropolis. To complicate matters, hot-tempered L'Enfant got himself into trouble by tearing down without permission a house that stood in the way of one of his avenues and that belonged to one of the leading citizens in the area; within a year of completing his stupendous plans, he had been dismissed. Little remembered, he lived on in genteel poverty until his death, in 1825.

As the first few government buildings went up, the unwelcome amount of empty space between them became an occasion for mockery, especially on the part of European visitors. Broad as the streets were, most of them remained unpaved and uncurbed during the early decades of the nineteenth century; hogs and fowl rooted and scratched by the wooden sidewalks that helped to mitigate for the wary pedestrian the hazards of winter ice, spring mud, and summer and autumn dust. For a long time, even the most desirable lots facing on

Above: At the New York City unveiling were Clare Boothe Luce, Robert W. Dowling, and Sol Hurok — respectively, a celebrated writer and political figure, a real-estate tycoon, and a highly successful theatrical impresario.

At right: Also at the New York City unveiling was the composer Richard Rodgers, photographed as he was introducing the US Ambassador to the United Nations, Ralph Bunche, who appears much amused by Rodgers' compliments.

In Washington, the model is shown to Mrs. Lyndon B. Johnson, wife of the then Vice-President of the United States, and to Mrs. Merriweather Post, a Washington philanthropist, as Roger L. Stevens looks on. The architect of the Center, Edward Durell Stone, greatly enjoyed displaying the model. He was a big, stoop-shouldered man, who spoke all his life with a strong Southern accent— he was born in Arkansas—practiced courtly, old-fashioned manners, and, like most successful members of his profession, was eager to charm clients into taking chances that were beyond their financial and aesthetic means. The Center as built is far less grandiose (and tens of millions of dollars less costly) than the structure that Stone had first hoped to construct upon the site.

the main avenues remained unsold; shanties were far more common throughout the city than mansions. Local boosters called Washington "the city of magnificent distances," but Charles Dickens, observing the scene in the eighteen-forties, apostrophized it as "the City of Magnificent Intentions."

To the critical eye, Washington until after the Civil War had the look of being an over-extended Southern market town, and it was only to be expected that its cultural resources were as meagre as its architecture. John Adams had written, "I must study politics and war that my sons may have liberty to study mathematics and philosophy ... in order to give their children a right to study painting, poetry, music, [and] architecture," but that hope was proving hard to fulfill; as far as the performing arts were concerned, it was well past the middle of the twentieth century before they were given an opportunity to flourish to a degree worthy of the city that Washington had by then become. The dating of this opportunity can be given precisely: it was the day—September 2nd—on which President Eisenhower signed the National Cultural Center Act of 1958.

Years of effort and weeks of congressional debate lay behind that pleasant occasion. The first step had been taken when, in 1955, President Eisenhower had appointed a District of Columbia Auditorium Commission to examine the feasibility of building a new auditorium in the capital and, if such an auditorium was feasible, to recommend a suitable location. The Commission was chaired by the redoubtable Agnes Meyer, and had among its members such prominent Washingtonians as Mrs. Robert Low Bacon and Frank Jelleff. In 1957, the Commission reported that a new auditorium was indeed feasible, and it recommended a site of some twenty-seven acres in Foggy Bottom, uphill from the river and including the land upon which the Kennedy Center was eventually built. By the time the report of the Commission had been digested and had reached a new embodiment in the form of a bill before Congress, most of the recommended site had been sold to private parties for commercial development. The leading champions of the Center in Congress were Frank Thompson, of New Jersey, in the House of Representatives, and J. William Fulbright, of Arkansas, in the Senate. In those days, Congress was skeptical of spending public moneys on the arts, and especially on the performing arts, and Thompson, Fulbright, and their allies, testifying before various committees of the House and Senate, had to place considerable emphasis upon the fact that the Center would be built and its subsequent programming paid for entirely by voluntary contributions from pri-

The model was also taken to the farm in Gettysburg, Pennsylvania, belonging to former President and Mrs. Eisenhower, where it met with their approval. Four years earlier, Eisenhower had signed the legislation that brought the Center into existence.

vate sources. The Center would be established under the benign umbrella of the Smithsonian Institution, but it would have its own officers and trustees, and the government would be asked to contribute nothing but its blessing and a suitable site. As things turned out, it was the seemingly simple matter of the site that nearly caused the entire project to founder, and not once but several times.

From the beginning, almost everyone concerned with what Senator Fulbright then called a National Capital Center for the Performing Arts had assumed that the ideal place for it would be facing the Mall directly across from the National Gallery. In the course of shepherding the Center through Congress, it was discovered that another worthy project under consideration there—a project for the building of what came to be known as the Air and Space Museum—was expected to occupy the very same site. Leading cultural organizations in Washington and throughout the country protested that the air museum should go anywhere *except* on the Mall, but the Museum had powerful sponsors; it became apparent that, in order to secure the establishment of the Center, its proponents would probably have to sacrifice the Mall site. Mrs. Bacon, of the Auditorium Commission, testified before Congress that there was still a sufficient amount of land available in Foggy Bottom to build the Center; her testimony was followed by that of a Washington attorney, Ralph E. Becker, who was then serving as chairman of the Cultural Development Committee of the Washington Board of Trade. Becker spoke ardently in favor of the Foggy Bottom site—a boomerang-shaped parcel of land comprising something under ten acres and lying directly across the Potomac from the wooded bird sanctuary of Theodore Roosevelt Island.

Becker, who became one of the original trustees of the Center and who served as its counsel from 1958 until 1976, had learned that the Foggy Bottom site could be acquired through a series of intricate negotiations with several interested parties, including the Navy, which controlled much of the land; the Department of the Interior, which had jurisdiction over Theodore Roosevelt Island; and the Board of Commissioners of the District of Columbia, which was eager to gain permission to erect at the southern tip of the island the supports for a new and much needed bridge linking certain District highways with highways on the Virginia shore— a project that had been held up for several years by conservationists and other interested parties. A skilled hand at the Washington art of multiple negotiations, Becker saw an opportunity to arrange a compromise that would leave all parties content and would insure for the Center what he regarded as an ideal location. He brought together Sherman Adams, President Eisenhower's chief of staff in the White House, and Fred Seaton, the Secretary of the Interior, and in a short time the problem of the placement of the supports for the bridge on Roosevelt Island was resolved. Next, David Finley, the chairman of the United States Commission of Fine Arts and a former director of the National Gallery, was called upon to form a committee to look over a number of possible sites and prepare a recommendation.

Finley and his committee, which included many distinguished local citizens, visited a total of seven sites and affirmed that the Foggy Bottom site was indeed the most appropriate one. After further give-and-take among various branches of government—for nothing is yielded in Washington without at least the semblance of a fierce struggle—and with much assistance from within the White House by Sherman Adams, the bill creating the Center was passed by Congress, and so it came about that within a matter of a few moments on September 2, 1958, President Eisenhower radically altered the entire future cultural life of Washington. Many years later, Eisenhower was honored by having one of the auditoriums in Kennedy Center named after him.

The Center existed on paper but without a penny in the till. Over a period of several months, it succeeded in accumulating a board of trustees, of whom half were *ex officio*—members of the Senate, the House of Representatives, the President's Cabinet, and the like—and half were private individuals, named by the President. Arthur Flemming, Secretary of Health, Education, and Welfare, was chosen to serve as the first chairman of the board and was succeeded by L. Corrin Strong, a Washington philanthropist, who was a former Ambassador to Norway and a close friend of Eisenhower's. Among the tasks that had to be carried out before a building could be erected were the squaring off of the awkwardly shaped site, the condemnation and pulling down of a few nondescript buildings on the site, the closing and demapping of portions of several streets, and the rerouting of a portion of the Rock Creek Parkway. Much of the cost of these tasks was borne by Ambassador Strong; he contributed nearly a million dollars to the Center between 1958 and 1961, when, following Kennedy's election to the Presidency and Eisenhower's retirement, Strong turned over the chairmanship of the board of the Center to Kennedy's appointee, Roger L. Stevens.

The board of trustees had already made a choice of an architect for the Center. They had been advised by friends who had observed the planning and construction of Lincoln Center, in New York City—a loosely linked complex of separate buildings, designed by a consortium of architects—that it would be more prudent to work with a single architect than with several, and their choice fell upon Edward Durell Stone, then approaching sixty and at the height of

Mamie Eisenhower and Jackie Kennedy in a sunny mood on the White House porch. Mrs. Eisenhower had come to tea to talk over plans for the Center and, indirectly, to let the world perceive that the Center was bipartisan in nature.

At right: President Kennedy applauds his wife after introducing her on a closed-circuit TV show that was broadcast to a paying audience in theatres from coast-to-coast as a means of helping to raise money for the construction of the Center. The event, which took place in the National Guard Armory, Washington, was called "An American Pageant of the Arts," and among the army of entertainers who pitched in to make the evening a success were Leonard Bernstein, Maria Tallchief, Jerome Robbins, Gene Kelly, Marian Anderson, and Benny Goodman.

his career. Stone was well known in architectural circles for his design (in collaboration with Philip Goodwin) of the Museum of Modern Art, in New York City, and for his design of the U.S. Embassy building, in New Delhi. He was a courtly, ebullient man and—like most architects—a born salesman. (The notorious eloquence of architects has caused many a client who wished to build a bungalow to end up paying for a castle.) Stone was delighted with the site and set about designing an elaborate, many-sided pavilion, with several auditoriums unfolding like the petals of some enormous flower from a central gathering place and fanning out onto a terrace that, among fountains and gardens, dropped gracefully down to the water's edge. It was a romantic structure, and while it was possible to approach it by land, the design implied that it would be best approached from the river, perhaps in some festively gilded and illuminated royal barge. Stone estimated the cost of the building at approximately seventy-five million dollars. The board accepted the design with speed; nothing remained but to turn it into a reality.

Soon two facts emerged: to raise seventy-five million dollars from the general public was going to be far more difficult than anyone had anticipated; moreover, given the constantly rising costs of construction, it was probably out of the question to build Stone's charming confection even for that substantial-seeming sum. When Roger L. Stevens accepted the chairmanship of the board and took a close look at the situation as it had been developing over the previous couple of years, he reported to President Kennedy that the Center might cost as much as a hundred million dollars. He recommended that Stone go back to the drawing board and work up plans for a much simpler and therefore much less expensive building—one that, with a minimum of architectural flourishes, would be able to carry out the mandate of the Center effectively.

This recommendation, which Kennedy accepted, was characteristic of Stevens: face a failed opportunity without regret and at once set about making new plans. In 1961, Stevens was fifty-one years old. He was well over six feet tall, with a handsome Roman head, made the more Roman by baldness and the less Roman by bright-blue eyes and an engaging smile. Having put on weight in the middle years, he was bigger than most other people, as well as taller, but his bigness suggested no threat; he moved at an unhurried pace, spoke so softly as to become, on some occasions, inaudible ("If I didn't know how to read lips," a friend of his has complained, "how on earth would I know what Roger was saying?"), and often he achieved his goals by sheer doggedness. People who had said "no" to him a dozen times would be astonished to find his blue eyes fastened upon them for a thirteenth or fourteenth time, and often enough they would feel inclined to give in at last and say "yes." He had a wife, Christine, who devoted much of her life to correcting mankind's habitually harsh treatment of animals, and a daughter, Christabel, who designed and made jewelry. He was active in three radically diverse fields, and in each of them he had gained a high reputation. He was one of the leading real-estate entrepreneurs in the country, he was perhaps the leading

President Kennedy greets a gathering of businessmen who, under the leadership of Ernest Breech, had been invited to Washington for the purpose of soliciting their aid in raising funds for the Center. Shaking hands with the President is Will Clayton; behind him are Paul Hoffman and Juan Trippe. A few weeks later, the President was dead.

theatrical producer on Broadway, and he was a superb political fund-raiser, especially in behalf of his friend Adlai Stevenson. Somehow, he had learned how to make money flow as if of its own accord in directions that were of his choosing.

A graduate of Choate School and a college dropout during the great Depression, Stevens had begun making money in real estate in his twenties; success followed success, and he became famous when, at forty-one, he negotiated a deal by which he and a number of colleagues purchased the Empire State Building, then the highest structure on earth and even today probably the most celebrated of all American skyscrapers. The purchase price was just over fifty million dollars, at that time the greatest sum ever paid for a single building. From that moment on, Stevens' name and that of the Empire State Building were indissolubly linked in the public view, but in the decade between 1951 and 1961 his primary interest shifted from real estate to the theatre; with an assortment of different partners, but often in partnership with Robert Whitehead, he produced such plays as "St. Joan," "Sabrina Fair," "Ondine," "Cat on a Hot Tin Roof," "Mary, Mary," "A Man For All Seasons," and "Bus Stop." He came to feel at ease in the world of arts and letters, which his curtailed schooling had left him alienated from; he took a far greater interest in intellectual pursuits than he did in increasing an already ample fortune. When Kennedy invited him to preside over the creation of the Center, Stevens perceived that it would give him an opportunity to employ his energy and skills in an area that had long been of importance to him. He accepted the chairmanship of the Center with the stipulation that he would serve without pay and with no perquisites except a car and driver. (After twenty years, that stipulation remains in effect.)

Working closely with Stevens, Stone drew up plans for a Center building that would embrace, under a single roof, three major auditoriums—an opera house, which, as built, contains twenty-three hundred seats; a concert hall, with twenty-seven hundred seats; and a legitimate theatre, with just over eleven hundred seats. Room was also found for a couple of smaller auditoriums, one of which was eventually to become the Terrace Theater—not completed until 1979—and a movie theatre designed to serve the needs of the American Film Institute, which first presented programming at the Center in 1973. The size of each of the three major auditoriums was determined not by the usual desire to achieve maximum revenues from maximum seating capacities but by taking the advice of experts as to the ideal sizes for such auditoriums. Halls that are bigger than they should be tend to fail not only acoustically but psychologically. As a Broadway producer, Stevens has always had a lively sense of the relationship between what is being performed and the space it is performed in; though a musical comedy, for example, might thrive in a theatre with sixteen hundred seats, a play by Edward Albee or Tennessee Williams would be likely to wither there.

Separating the three major auditoriums were two immense halls, running from the broad

Over the years, many actors and actresses took part in events intended to call public attention to the long-awaited Center. Here Alfred Drake, celebrated as one of the stars of the Cole Porter musical "Kiss Me, Kate," appears on a TV program entitled "Creative America" over CBS in March, 1963. At right: Helen Hayes appears on a TV program over NBC in the summer of 1964. A native of Washington, Miss Hayes has long been an ardent champion of the Center.

On May 13, 1964, in the Cabinet Room at the White House, Stevens is sworn in as Special Assistant to the President on the Arts—a post he was to hold until Nixon succeeded Johnson in the presidency.

Below: Groundbreaking for the Center on a blustery day in December, 1964. The gold-plated spade, with which President Johnson performed the traditional rite, had first been used by President McKinley, in 1898, to plant a scarlet oak on the front lawn of the White House. In 1914, President Taft had broken ground with it for the Lincoln Memorial, and President Franklin Delano Roosevelt had used it for a similar purpose, in 1938, to mark the beginning of construction at the Jefferson Memorial. Roger L. Stevens is at left, standing in front of his now familiar companion, the model of the Center. Among others looking on are Mrs. Johnson, Robert Kennedy (later a Center trustee), and two of his sisters, Jean Kennedy Smith (later a Center trustee) and Eunice Shriver.

The celebrated actor Sir John Gielgud, somewhat disguised in a Navy pea jacket and mink cap, reciting a few lines from Shakespeare's "Henry V." Jason Robards, Jr. (second from right), having left his notes on the plane that had brought him to Washington, quoted from memory remarks concerning artists and the arts that President Kennedy had made on several occasions.

entrance driveway on the land side of the building to a Grand Foyer on the river side. This foyer was to be six hundred feet long, forty feet wide, and sixty feet high, making it one of the largest rooms in the country, if not in the world; the three auditoriums opened upon it, and during intermissions several thousand people would be able to stroll about in comfort, mingling with friends and being served drinks from a number of convenient portable bars. Under the main floor of the Center was a garage on three levels, capable of holding fourteen hundred cars. Visitors to the Center would be able to drive into the garage, park, and make their way up to their destinations by escalator, protected from extremes of heat, cold, and stormy weather. The building would contain restaurants, a cafeteria, and an assortment of reception rooms of different sizes, in which parties could be held for distinguished visitors. In the backstage areas would be found the most advanced technical equipment and the most spacious actors' dressing rooms of any theatrical establishment in the country. The entire building would be heated and cooled by electricity—by far the largest installation of its kind ever devised.

Renderings of the exterior of the building showed a severely rectangular box, six hundred and thirty feet long, three hundred feet wide, and a hundred feet high. A broad colonnade encircled all four sides of the building; the roof of the colonnade was supported by tapering metal posts, which paid indirect tribute, in a contemporary form, to the nearby Lincoln Memorial and the other classical, many-pillared buildings in Washington. The Center would be clad from top to bottom in pure white marble, also in tribute to the favored color and favored stone of the city. The upper surface of the roof of the colonnade would serve as an enormous terrace, from which a spectacular view of Washington would be gained; from the colonnade itself, readily accessible through the lofty glass doors of the Grand Foyer, a terrace was cantilevered out into space above a concealed highway; from this terrace one could look out on a summer's night to the hushed river, the dark greenness of Roosevelt Island, and the twinkling lights of the Virginia shore.

If the new design was less opulent and less romantic than its predecessor, it was surely far more efficient. Big as it was, it would be placed in the midst of a rolling parkland, which, with the eventual growth of trees and shrubs, would help to disguise its formidable bulk. The facade of the Center, unlike that of its toothily crenellated neighbor-to-be, the Watergate Hotel and Apartments, would be unadorned, and despite the thousands of visitors that the Center would be capable of entertaining daily, it was expected to strike a note of what the ever-lyrical Stone called "idyllic repose in one of the most glorious settings in the world."

Edward Durell Stone and Roger L. Stevens at a press conference in late 1965. Construction is getting under way at the site, and a need for more money forces the Center to make itself well known even before the first performance can be given there.

Upper left: Again and again, Stevens had to go up to "the Hill" to discuss the financing of the Center with members of Congress. Many of them were doubtful that government should have anything to do with whatever was implied by "culture," and of all the arts the performing arts were certainly the most suspect. Here Stevens is testifying before a Congressional Committee in May, 1969.

Upper right: Mr. and Mrs. Stevens attend the opening of a concert in Constitution Hall in the autumn of 1967.

Henry James wrote once that, everything being equal, a building that sits is more pleasing than a building that stands; the Center would undoubtedly sit, with an imperturbability akin to that of the White House and National Gallery—structures that emerge from the landscape in a fashion traditional to a largely horizontal city.

The trustees having approved the new design, a model of the Center was officially unveiled at a ceremony held at the home of President Kennedy's mother-in-law, Mrs. Hugh D. Auchincloss, in Newport, Rhode Island, in the early fall of 1962. A few days later, the model travelled to the farm home of the Eisenhowers, in Gettysburg, Pennsylvania, where the former President gave it his endorsement. Stevens felt confident that Stone had devised a building that, even in the face of constantly rising costs, could be erected for something over thirty million dollars; nevertheless, difficulties remained. For one thing, there was prolonged quarreling over the correctness of the choice of a site—quarreling that Stevens was to listen to, with mounting impatience, for several years to come. Certain self-appointed urbanologists held that the site was too far from the center of town; others held that there would be no ready means of access to it because of the spaghetti of highways surrounding it; and still others prophesied that, being put up on filled land, the Center might someday give way and topple sidelong into the Potomac, if by then the Potomac had not risen in an unprecedented flood and washed it downriver and so out to sea.

Another difficulty involved an awkward linking of time and money. According to the terms of the 1958 act establishing the Center as nominally a bureau of the Smithsonian, if funds sufficient to build the Center were not in hand by the end of five years, then such funds as had been raised were to be turned over to the Smithsonian and the Center terminated. When Stevens took over the chairmanship, approximately three million dollars had been raised, some of which had already been spent. It had become evident that Washington, although it would be the most direct beneficiary of the Center and although it was known to be the home of many wealthy individuals, would contribute only a negligible fraction of the total sum needed. Stevens cheerfully confessed to being a carpetbagger, brought down from New York City to perform a task that no Washington resident appeared willing or able to perform. By an irony, the Center's receiving so little support as a local organization would direct its focus wholly on fulfilling its congressional mandate to become a national one.

Stevens vigorously set about gaining grants from foundations and corporations throughout the country. In November, 1962, the most ambitious of all the Center's fund-raising projects took place—a spectacular called "An American Pageant of the Arts" was broadcast on closed-circuit TV to ticket-holders from coast to coast. It was hoped that the show would net the Center from three to five million dollars—far less (roughly half a million) was realized, but

Completion of the first major segment of construction was celebrated with a topping out in late January, 1968. Trustees Mary Lasker and Erich Leinsdorf, and other dignitaries, signed their names to a steel violoncello. In September, 1968, steel masks of comedy and tragedy were hoisted over the present Eisenhower Theater to signal completion of the superstructure.

invaluable prominence for the concept of the Center was achieved. Skeptics—many of them members of Congress—began to ask whether the national eagerness to possess a cultural center was any greater than that which had been manifested by the residents of Washington. Despite much grumbling, in 1963 Congress granted the Center an extension of five years in which to achieve its financial goals. At that moment, the Center had raised a total of about twelve million dollars—not a small sum but one that was radically incommensurate with the Center's needs. Stevens labored bravely on, arguing the case for the Center with his usual diffident, invincible persuasiveness.

Meanwhile, the situation was somewhat less bleak than it looked, thanks to an unpublicized agreement that had been reached between Kennedy and his Secretary of the Interior, Stewart Udall. It was estimated that the substructure of the Center, including the three-story-high garage, would cost approximately fifteen million dollars to build, while the superstructure, which contained all the auditoriums, would cost approximately thirty-one million dollars. The Department of the Interior consented to advance money for the erection of the substructure, which upon completion would begin to generate large sums of money from parking fees. No such sums were likely to arise from the activities that would be taking place in the superstructure; on the contrary, the performing arts are, and nearly always have been, a deficit operation. For that reason, at the October, 1963, luncheon at the White House, during which Kennedy deplored the absence of a suitable cultural center in the nation's capital, he suggested to his businessmen-guests that a hundred of the biggest corporations in America might be willing to make a substantial contribution—say, a hundred thousand dollars apiece—toward the construction of the superstructure. Kennedy and the businessmen got along well at the luncheon, which ended with an informal proposal that this unprecedented gesture on the part of American corporations (for in the early nineteen-sixties business and the arts were by no means as closely wedded as they are today) would be announced at a dinner to be held at the White House in January or February of the coming year.

On the evening of the day that Kennedy was assassinated, Stevens and several other trustees of the Center, including the well-known philanthropist Mary Lasker, spoke of their shock and sorrow over the death of the man whose belief in the future of the Center had been a major source of encouragement to them. After a time, their talk turned to the question of some form of permanent memorial to Kennedy; what could be more suitable than to name the Center after him? LeMoyne Billings, also a trustee of the Center and one of Kennedy's closest friends, was staying at the White House, and within a few hours of the conclusion of the obsequies at Arlington Billings saw to it that a formal proposal regarding the Center was presented to Stephen Smith, Arthur Schlesinger, Jr., and Larry O'Brien, representing the Kennedy family, and to Mike Feldman, representing President Lyndon Johnson. Feldman assured the group that Johnson would do everything in his power to carry out the Kennedy family's wishes, whatever they might prove to be. Billings next carried the proposal to the family itself. He learned that another possible memorial to Kennedy in Washington was already under consideration: it had been suggested that the name of Pennsylvania Avenue be changed to Kennedy Avenue. Billings argued against this, pointing out that the Center would serve as a living embodiment for all time of Kennedy's strong belief in the importance of the arts in American life. After further discussions that evening and the following day, the Kennedy family accepted the proposal, as well as the stipulation, ardently championed by Billings, that the Center should be the only memorial to Kennedy in the capital; like the Washington Monument and the Lincoln and Jefferson Memorials, it would enjoy the privilege of singularity.

The next step was to seek the approval of Congress. After several joint hearings held over a period of several weeks, a bill—the John F. Kennedy Center Act—was drawn up to amend the original National Cultural Center Act of 1958. By an intricate system of matching gifts and long-term bond issues, some of them already in place and others newly devised, the federal government would make up the difference between the twelve million dollars the Center had in hand and the approximately forty-six million dollars that was the estimated cost of the Center. The new act—Public Law 88-260—was passed by Congress on January 10, 1964, and was signed thirteen days later by President Johnson. The act contained the following eloquent preamble:

Whereas the late John Fitzgerald Kennedy served with distinction as President of the United States, and as a Member of the Senate and House of Representatives; and

Whereas the late John Fitzgerald Kennedy dedicated his life to the advancement of the welfare of mankind; and

Construction of the building was plagued by many delays, but in the spring of 1969 one could see that the broad "pod" of the underground garage, upon which the Center proper was to stand, had been largely finished and that concrete was being poured for the immense flat roof of the Center, sealing it off from the noise of jet planes landing and leaping skyward at the nearby National Airport. The excavation in the foreground was for the Watergate apartments; nobody knew at the time that "Watergate" would one day enter the language, not as a synonym for luxurious living but for clumsy and unsuccessful political skullduggery.

At right: A view of the Opera House under construction, looking down from the top of the fly loft. The successful production of operas requires an exceptionally large backstage space, both vertical and horizontal.

The Center nearing completion. The approaches, whether to the garage or to the formal entrances on the upper level on the north side of the building, remain unfinished, and the open land around the Center has the look of a much fought-over battlefield, but the hardest part of the task has been accomplished. In the background stands part of the newly erected Watergate complex.

Whereas the late John Fitzgerald Kennedy was particularly devoted to the advancement of the performing arts within the United States; and

Whereas by his untimely death this Nation and the world has suffered a great loss; and

Whereas it is the sense of the Congress that it is only fitting and proper that a suitable monument be dedicated to the memory of this great leader; and

Whereas the living memorial to be named in his honor by this joint resolution shall be the sole national monument to his memory within the city of Washington and its environs.

It was not until December 2, 1964, that Stevens was ready to hold a ground-breaking ceremony at the Center. By then, Stone's working drawings had been completed, much of the site had been bulldozed into a shapely, uninterruptedly open hillside, and still another round of suggestions for presumably superior sites had been faced and outwitted. (With understandable irritation, Stevens was quoted in the Washington *Post* as saying, "In discussions with those who would change the site, I have yet to be asked to consider a specific location which is both suitable and available.") December is by no means an ideal month for breaking ground, but Stevens was eager to establish the Center as an unchallengeable presence in the place where it was going to be and thus put an end to any further local criticism, whether amateur or professional. As a builder, Stevens was aware that a yawning hole in the ground is a powerful argument and a steel frame is irrefutable.

The second of December happened to be an especially cold and windy day, and the group that gathered on a temporary platform in Foggy Bottom to observe the first spadeful of dirt being turned by President Johnson were well bundled up against the weather. (One old Kennedy friend, Justice of the Supreme Court Byron R. White, took care to wear a heavy overcoat beneath his judicial robes.) Besides the Johnsons and Vice-President-Elect and Mrs. Humphrey, among those present were Senator-Elect and Mrs. Robert Kennedy, Senator and Mrs. Edward Kennedy, Mrs. Stephen Smith, Mrs. Sargent Shriver (both sisters of the late President), Arthur M. Schlesinger, Jr., the Stevenses, the Stones, and Mrs. Auchincloss, whom President Johnson thanked for her money-raising activities on behalf of the Center.

The gold-plated shovel that President Johnson thrust vigorously into the ground had first been used by President McKinley, in 1898, for the purpose of planting a tree on the front lawn of the White House. In 1914, President Taft had used it to break ground for the building of the Lincoln Memorial, and President Roosevelt had made use of it for the same purpose in 1938, in the building of the Jefferson Memorial. President Johnson said that the Center would "symbolize our belief that the world of creation and thought are at the core of all civilization." He added that the role of government at the Center must necessarily be a small one, since "no Act of Congress or Executive Order can call a great musician or poet into existence." Robert Kennedy spoke of his brother's belief "that America is judged as every civilization is judged—in large measure, by the quality of its artistic achievement." President Johnson then called upon witnesses from what he called "the worlds of poetry and power." Among them was Sir John Gielgud, who, formidably disguised in a Navy pea jacket, a mink cap, and black-rimmed spectacles, recited a passage from Shakespeare's "Henry V." Jason Robards, Jr., confessing that he had left his notes for the occasion aboard the plane that had brought him to Washington, quoted from memory words in which President Kennedy had once praised the career of André Malraux, French Minister of Cultural Affairs: "'In his life, he has demonstrated that politics and art, the life of action and the world of thought, the world of events and the world of imagination, are one.'"

After the lofty, encouraging words spoken at the ground-breaking ceremonies, one might have expected the Center to proceed without difficulties to a speedy conclusion. In fact, the darkest days of the project lay ahead. With good luck, a structure the size of the Center would be likely to take two or three years to erect; the Center took over six. There were many reasons that things went badly instead of well. Certain events over which the Center had no control required alterations in the architectural plans; perhaps the most important of these events was the granting of permission for jets to fly in and out of the National Airport, only a short distance away from the Center. At great cost, the concrete roof and glass doors of the Center had to be insulated against the jets' high volume of sound. Other alterations in the plans were the result of a substantial underestimation of costs; the steelwork alone cost a couple of million dollars more than had been anticipated. Meanwhile, there were labor disputes on and off the site, which led directly and indirectly to long delays in the delivery of materials. For example, marble from Carrara, a gift of the Italian government, was held up for several months by a maritime strike. Moreover, the Center, though a quasi-private institution, was being constructed under the supervision of the federal government, and the usual miles of strangling—and time-consuming—red tape were not to be circumvented.

Worst of all was a perennial shortage of cash in hand. Stevens and his colleagues found themselves constantly obliged to beg for money, not only from private sources but from Congress as well, and Congress grew increasingly restive with every new appeal. From the beginning, there had been considerable skepticism in Congress in respect to the wisdom of the government's undertaking to finance any aspect of the arts. The Center had been an experiment in such funding; the Endowment for the Arts and the Endowment for the Humanities followed a trail that the Center had been the first to blaze (which is why it was natural, in 1964, to ask Stevens to serve as the first chairman of the National Council on the Arts, the parent body of the Endowment for the Arts. He held the office through 1969). Congress had consented to allot substantial sums to the Center under the spur of Kennedy's death, but as the years passed the spur diminished in effectiveness and more and more voices were heard pro-

At left: On May 27, 1971, a gala preview of the Center raised nearly a quarter of a million dollars to establish funding for the Specially Priced Ticket Program. During the past decade, over a million eligible patrons—students, enlisted military, and elderly and handicapped persons—have attended performances at half-price.

George London and Julius Rudel served as, respectively, Artistic Administrator and Music Adviser of the Center during its formative years.

testing that the Center was little more than a colossal boondoggle. Patiently, Stevens went up to the Capitol and explained—not for the first time, not for the last—the Center's ever-increasing financial needs. At the same time, he was doing his best to juggle such funds as had already come into his possession. As a real-estate man, he was accustomed to making time work for him instead of against him; tenaciously, he kept applying pressure, and one of his friends, observing him in action during this period, described him as having the force of a glacier making its way slowly down through some narrow Alpine pass. "Sometimes it was difficult," the friend has said, "to tell whether the glacier or the mountain pass would suffer the most, but always it was certain that Roger would have his way."

There were moments of gloom that had nothing to do with difficulties of constructing the Center and in raising the funds to pay for that construction, for throughout the entire period of its gestation the Center was constantly under challenge in regard to the fulfillment of its mandate to become a national and not a local center for the performing arts. Countless articles in newspapers and magazines, as well as discussions on radio and TV, demanded to know how the feat of representing an entire country in a single place—even if that place were the nation's capital—would be accomplished. If the Center was to be a national institution, what would be its relations with the organizations already in existence in Washington? Would it found a new opera company or be content to join forces with the old? Similar inquiries were made in regard to the local symphony orchestra and the local ballet company. Would the Center launch its own acting company, or would it invite companies from other cities to come and play limited engagements? Stevens and his colleagues answered these and other questions with answers as indefinite as possible; the options for the Center were many and it was important to keep them open for as long as possible.

An especially persistent speculation in the press was whether it would turn out that the Center, despite its high ambitions for itself, would end up as little more than a booking agent for conventional theatrical activities, which would presumably make money for the Center but would have no interest in fostering new and perhaps risky experiments in the arts. Scores of so-called think pieces on this subject were written, and if they served any useful purpose it was that of obliging the Center to come to grips with its future well before that future arrived. The world of arts is full of surprises both pleasant and unpleasant, and only by dint of shrewd anticipatory gambles can one reduce the number of probable disappointments. The executive staff of the Center underwent several major changes before the Center opened as well as afterward; these changes reflected the usual difficulties attendant upon the launching of a new and exceptionally complex enterprise and were by no means entirely negative. For one thing, they led to a sharpening of focus in regard to the capacities of the Center—a process aided by the building itself, which as it neared completion began to assert, as buildings have a way of doing, a personality of its own. The transformation of blueprints into stone, bronze, and glass amounted to a series of discoveries, some of which were welcome (sufficient space was found, for example, in the backstage area of the Eisenhower Theater to carve out a small movie theatre for the American Film Institute) and some of which were unwelcome. (Far too little office space had been provided for the Center's staff, which, small though it was, had to learn over the years to live like moles in a patchwork labyrinth. Luckily, Stevens, unlike most executives, paid little attention to the trappings of his position; he appeared unaware that his bleak, windowless box of an office lacked what it might so easily have had—a superb view of the Potomac flowing a few hundred feet beyond his desk.)

The official opening date of the Center had to be postponed several times. Long before the opening, on September 8, 1971, the public was enjoying at least partial access to the building and to the grounds. For the Center was a memorial as well as a place of entertainment, and even in its unfinished state it became a favorite point of interest to tourists visiting Washington. In the weeks following the opening, they poured through the building by the tens of thousands, bringing favorable word of it back to their home towns all over America. Despite the doubts so often expressed by Congress and by critics in the press, and despite the grumblings about the General Services Administration, which had overseen its long-drawn-out construction, the Center, having thrown open its doors at last, moved quickly to fulfill its destiny.

Perhaps the most convincing measure of the national—and even international—importance of the opening ceremonies was the fact that the New York *Times*, on the morning of September 9, chose to spread a photograph of the event over five columns of its front page. The photograph showed Leonard Bernstein embracing Mrs. Joseph P. Kennedy, and the story that accompanied it, written by Nan Robertson, began on a note of excited rhetoric rare in the *Times*:

The capital of this nation finally strode into the Cultural Age tonight with the spectacular opening of the $70 million John F. Kennedy Center for the Performing Arts.

The rich, celebrated, and powerful flocked to the world premiere of Leonard Bernstein's Mass in the gigantic marble temple to music, dance, and drama on the Potomac's edge.

The Kennedy family, led by Mrs. Joseph P. Kennedy, filled the choicest boxes in the Center's Opera House. Mrs. Kennedy's only surviving son, Senator Edward M. Kennedy, attended her in Box No. 1 with his wife, Joan; Aaron Copland, the composer; Walter E. Washington, the capital city's Mayor, and Mrs. Washington and the Bernsteins.

Only Mrs. Aristotle Onassis, widow of the assassinated President for whom the Center has been named, was not there to hear the premiere of the work she had requested from Mr. Bernstein. She decided not to attend only last week.

Despite her absence, emotion peaked tonight after previews Monday and last night in which Mr. Bernstein wept during tumultuous ovations and some members of the audience were also moved to tears. Called "a theatre piece for singers, dancers, and players," the Mass lasts almost two hours and includes a cast of 200 that fills the stage and orchestra pit.

The account in the *Times* went on to say that the evening had begun with the dimming of the lights in the Opera House, whereupon Stevens had strode out upon the stage—a tall, smiling man, who even when he smiles has always managed to preserve his air of Roman gravity. What was he thinking as he stood there, after so many years of effort, so many challenges met, so many defeats outwitted? Characteristically, he offered no clue; from the *Times*:

Mrs. George Garrett (center), an early supporter and trustee of the Center and its first Honorary Trustee, is flanked by Mrs. Clayton Fritchey and Ambassadors Llewellyn Thompson and Charles Bohlen, and their wives, at the Founders Day Luncheon of the Friends of the Kennedy Center, held in the Grand Foyer in 1971.

Mr. Stevens stood quietly while being given a standing ovation, then welcomed the guests. He noted that the Center was dedicated as the only memorial to John F. Kennedy in Washington and that Mr. Kennedy had "more than any predecessor" as President "lent dignity to the role of the arts and their place in society."

In one of several other stories in the *Times*, Howard Taubman quoted President Kennedy as saying, "I look forward to an America which commands respect throughout the world not only for its strength but for its civilization as well. I see little of more importance for the future of our country and our civilization than the full recognition of the place of the artist." Taubman noted that "Roger L. Stevens, Chairman of the Board, and Julius Rudel, the Center's music director, have said repeatedly that they wanted the programming [of the Center] to be creative. With the three opening productions in the Opera House—Leonard Bernstein's new 'Mass', Alberto Ginastera's new opera, 'Beatrix Cenci,' and the new production of Handel's rarely heard opera, 'Ariodante'—they have offered proof of their willingness to be adventurous."

As a gesture of courtesy to the Kennedy family, President Nixon had refrained from making an appearance on the first of what amounted to a series of opening nights; on the second night, he and Mrs. Nixon occupied the Presidential box in the Concert Hall. Conducted by Antal Dorati, the National Symphony Orchestra played a program that consisted of Beethoven's "Consecration of the House Overture," written over a century and a half ago for the opening of the Josephstadt Theatre, in Vienna; Mozart's Violin Concerto No. 3 in G major; Stravinsky's "Rite of Spring"; and William Schuman's "Secular Cantata No. 2, A Free Song." The last selection amounted to an act of homage to the composer, who, along with his wife, was a guest of the Nixons in the Presidential box; also present were Mr. and

The opening of the Eisenhower Theater in the Kennedy Center took place on October 18, 1971, in the presence of President and Mrs. Nixon and Mr. and Mrs. John Eisenhower. The play was Ibsen's "A Doll's House," starring Claire Bloom.

Mrs. Stevens and Mr. David Lloyd Kreeger, a generous benefactor of the National Symphony Orchestra, with his wife.

From that triumphant first week of the Center's existence up to the present day, the various auditoriums of the Center have welcomed one historically significant artistic event after another. Artists have come to perform at the Center from every corner of the nation and, indeed, of the globe. From the start, it was evident that the Center, unlike nearly every other cultural center that had been built up to that time, was a highly efficient servant of the arts. The great bulk of its exterior was often derided—it was called a Brobdingnagian shoebox, a beached whale, the world's largest Kleenex box, and other reproachful nicknames—but its interior spaces were constantly praised, both for their comparatively modest appropriateness of size and for their admirable acoustics, designed by Dr. Cyril Harris. The only substantial physical defect in the building were a persistently leaky roof and terraces which were made weatherproof at last in 1978. (In contrast, three of the main buildings of Lincoln Center—Avery Fisher Hall, the New York State Theatre, and the Vivian Beaumont Theatre—have been, or are about to be, rebuilt, at a cost of many millions of dollars, to remedy structural and acoustic defects.) To the general astonishment, Washington, so long described as a cultural wasteland, began to obtain aesthetic plums that hitherto had been reserved solely for New York; there were even certain plums that, on being offered a choice between the two cities, chose Washington over New York.

Symptomatic of this unexpected rivalry was the fact that the Teatro alla Scala, coming from Milan to the United States for the first time in its history, gave its operatic performances at the Center and left New York to satisfy itself with a Verdi Requiem. The Vienna State Opera followed a similar course. Much of the credit for these and other important "scoops" goes to Martin Feinstein, who served as Executive Director for the Performing Arts at the

Center during its crucial early years. Julius Rudel was also a highly valued shaper of the Center's destiny at a time when the world of entertainment remained skeptical both of the seriousness of the Center's intentions and of its ability to carry them out. Between them, Feinstein and Rudel knew dozens and even hundreds of the most significant figures in that world, and they saw to it that the Center profited daily from this knowledge. Many of the tasks that Feinstein and Rudel carried out are now in the hands of Marta Istomin, wife of the pianist Eugene Istomin, who bears the title of Artistic Director of the Center, and who is in charge of programming for all of the performing arts with the exception of theatre. Increasingly, ballet critics found themselves having to journey to the Center to observe performances of distinguished dance companies both foreign and domestic. As for the theatre, one of the most sophisticated dramatists now writing in English, Tom Stoppard, was soon drawing larger and more sympathetic audiences at the Center than he was on Broadway. In the Concert Hall, performances were given by artists as celebrated and as radically unlike in their gifts as Arthur Rubinstein, Duke Ellington, Isaac Stern, Dietrich Fischer-Dieskau, Andrés Segovia, Jean-Pierre Rampal, Luciano Pavarotti, Count Basie, and Aaron Copland.

Before the Center was built, it was sometimes predicted that it might prove an elitist organization; after it had been in operation for a few years, it was sometimes accused of being too popular for its own good. Management has been able to face these contradictory propositions with equanimity. In the Center's early years, it was of critical importance to establish a substantial local audience, as well as to call attention to the Center's existence nationally and internationally. Judging this task to have been largely accomplished, in recent years the Center has been devoting a larger and larger portion of its resources to what it calls its Section 4 activities. These activities have to do with public service and education, as defined in Section 4 of the congressional statute that authorized the Center, and many are under the supervision of Thomas R. Kendrick, Director of Operations. In 1981, well over two and a half million

William McCormick Blair, Jr. (center), General Director of the Kennedy Center from 1968 to 1972, standing with the Swiss Ambassador Felix Schnyder and the Swiss sculptor Willy Weber at a ceremony marking the presentation, as a gift from the Swiss government, of Weber's abstract stainless-steel sculpture "Apollo Ten, 1970."

dollars, raised by the Center from private sources, will be allocated for the funding of such Section 4 activities as the following:

(1) The maintenance of a specially priced ticket program, by means of which up to fifteen per cent of the tickets to regular performances are made available, at half price, to students, handicapped persons, persons over sixty-five, low-income groups, and enlisted military personnel. In fiscal 1980, about a hundred and ten thousand tickets were sold through this program which would have resulted in total additional gross income of seven hundred and ninety-five thousand dollars.

(2) Free events. In 1980, more than two hundred thousand people attended a total of five hundred public-service events at the Center, including special performances, symposia, lectures, and exhibitions.

(3) Expanded participation in the performing arts by black, Hispanic, and other ethnic groups, both at the Center and throughout the country. Since 1978, more than seven hundred

Pablo Casals and Alexander Schneider at the Center on May 22, 1973. The occasion was a gala concert commemorating the twenty-fifth anniversary of the Charter of the Organization of American States. The concert was part of the Fifth Inter-American Festival, held annually at the Center. Casals was to have conducted the "Gloria" from his composition "El Pessebre." Unluckily, he was taken ill and Schneider conducted in his place. Casals was able to appear with Schneider at the end of the concert; he was then ninety-six years of age.

On November 14, 1980, in honor of the eightieth birthday of Aaron Copland, the National Symphony Orchestra played his "Lincoln Portrait," with Leonard Bernstein conducting and Copland serving as the most appropriate of narrators.

thousand dollars have been spent upon a score of successful ventures, among them a National Black Theatre and Playwright Project, which assisted in the production of eight new plays in six black regional theatres, and a National Black Music Colloquium and Competition, encouraging the composition and performance of music by black composers.

(4) The Terrace Theater, a three-million-dollar Bicentennial gift from the government and people of Japan, is the local home of The Acting Company (founded in 1972, by John Houseman and Margot Harley), which is the Center's officially designated national touring theatre company. The Terrace Theater is also the home of the Theatre Chamber Players, the Center's resident chamber-music group; of the Center's Programs for Children and Youth; and of the American College Theatre Festival. Since it began operations in 1979, the Terrace Theater has presented well over eight hundred performances by a hundred and fifty different theatre, dance, and musical groups from all sections of the country.

(5) The Theater Lab, an experimental-theatre space operated by the Center. The Lab concerns itself with the development of new musical and theatrical works and is also the site throughout the year of free play readings and a variety of programs for children.

(6) The Performing Arts Library is a joint undertaking with the Library of Congress, which which contains the nation's most comprehensive collection of books, movies, recordings, and other materials having to do with the performing arts. The resources of this collection are instantly available to users of the Center library by means of video computers. The library's own collection of books and theatrical memorabilia is also readily accessible, much of it upon open shelves. A well-lighted, comfortably furnished retreat on the top floor of the Center, the library was designed by Philip Johnson and John Burgee, as was the Terrace Theater—ironically, a space highly praised by the very architectural critics who, a decade ago, were deploring the

unnecessary vastness of the Center building. If the Center had not been so vast, sufficient room for the library, the Terrace Theater, the American Film Institute Theatre, and the Theater Lab could never have been found within its walls.

The chief components of the Kennedy Center's Education Program are four in number, to wit:

(1) The annual American College Theatre Festival, which in 1981 involved more than four hundred colleges and universities in thirteen regional festivals and a three-week-long National Festival at the Center. The budget for the Center amounts to just over half a million dollars, of which more than half is raised from corporations and other private sources.

(2) The Alliance for Arts Education, a joint project with the United States Department of Education. Its purpose is to foster the integration of the arts into every child's education. AAE committees in each state coöperate with local departments of education to draw up and implement plans for arts education in the schools. The AAE provides a method of communication among interested parties on a local, state, and national level and operates on a budget of two hundred thousand dollars.

(3) The Programs for Children and Youth, a model performing-arts program at the Center. A National Children's Arts Festival is conducted annually at the Center, and key elements are presented in selected cities throughout the country; in 1981, outreach festivals were held in Birmingham, Milwaukee, and Seattle. Teacher workshops, conferences, and

*Above: Standing at attention during
the singing of the National Anthem
are President and Mrs. Carter along
with Fred Astaire, Marian Anderson,
Richard Rodgers, Arthur Rubinstein,
and George Balanchine. (Mrs. Polk
Guest and Mrs. Rodgers are also present.)*

*Far left: Stevens and President Ford,
backstage at the Opera House on
September 4, 1974, greet the cast of
David Merrick's "Mack and Mabel"
(left to right, Lisa Kirk, Robert Preston,
and Bernadette Peters).*

*At right: President and Mrs. Reagan
congratulating Elizabeth Taylor on
the opening night at the Center of a
new production of "The Little Foxes"
(March 19, 1981). The author of the play,
Lillian Hellman, is seen at the left.*

demonstration projects are conducted jointly with the National Committee, Arts for the Handicapped, which is an educational affiliate of the Center. The budget for 1981 is approximately half a million dollars.

(4) Arts Coalition Northwest, a regional organization set up to serve the states of Washington, Oregon, Montana, Idaho, and Alaska. This pilot project is being carried out in coöperation with the Seattle Center and is designed to support activities in the performing arts in a number of different fields. If it proves successful, similar regional coalitions will be established throughout the rest of the country. Its budget is one hundred and fifty thousand dollars.

Under the leadership of Mrs. Lily Guest, an organization called the Friends of the Kennedy Center has attained a membership of almost seven thousand people. The Friends present weekly symposia at the Center; among the prominent figures who have participated in these symposia are Tennessee Williams, Isaac Stern, Mary Martin, and Marcia Haydée. Nearly three hundred Friends serve, on a volunteer basis, as tour guides at the Center and as attendants at the Center's information booth and souvenir shop. The Friends contribute a total of more than sixty-five thousand hours a year to the Center—a gift of time that has been valued at more than a quarter of a million dollars. Proceeds from the dues paid by the Friends and from the sale of souvenirs go to finance educational and public-service programs.

The major source of financing for all such programs is the Corporate Fund for the Performing Arts at Kennedy Center. Founded in 1977, the Fund has been described as a "voluntary group of American business leaders committed to the support of the Kennedy Center as a national cultural treasure." In 1980, it raised one and three-quarters million dollars, and it is clear that even larger sums will be required in the future, as the national responsibilities of the Center continue to increase.

For a number of years, the Center appeared to preserve a wary distance between itself and television, but ever since 1978, when an annual event entitled "Kennedy Center Honors: A National Celebration of the Performing Arts" was inaugurated at the Center and broadcast over CBS-TV, the relationship has been growing warmer. Almost overnight, "Kennedy Center Honors" achieved a high place in the cultural life of the country, perhaps because the operating principle behind it is so simple and just. Five persons are chosen each year by the Board of Trustees of the Center to be honored for their lifelong devotion to one or another of the performing arts. In 1978, the honors list included Marian Anderson, Fred Astaire, George Balanchine, Richard Rodgers, and Arthur Rubinstein; in 1979, it included Aaron Copland, Ella Fitzgerald, Henry Fonda, Martha Graham, and Tennessee Williams, and in 1980 Leonard Bernstein, James Cagney, Agnes de Mille, Lynn Fontanne, and Leontyne Price. (Mr. Bernstein characteristically protested, only half in jest, that he and Miss Price were far too young to be honored; after all, he said, they were still engaged in making their careers.) In 1981, the honorees are Count Basie, Cary Grant, Helen Hayes, Jerome Robbins, and Rudolf Serkin. "Kennedy Center Honors" having proved a success on commercial TV, in 1981 a series of regularly scheduled shows called "Kennedy Center Tonight!" was launched, sponsored in part by the Shell Companies Foundation and in part by the Corporation for

Public Broadcasting. On the first show, Leonard Bernstein, Hal Holbrook, and Mstislav Rostropovich paid tribute to Aaron Copland on the occasion of his eightieth birthday; the second show devoted itself to the memory of Duke Ellington; and the third show celebrated the life and times of Sarah Bernhardt, as performed by Lilli Palmer.

September, 1981: the tenth anniversary of the opening of the Kennedy Center—like any birthday, a time for simultaneously looking back and looking forward. The success of the Center can be measured on many scales, the most obvious of which is the statistical. Since 1971, over forty million people from all over the world have visited the Center. A third of them have been ticket holders, who have attended a total of ten thousand performances on one or another of the Center's stages. More than a million people have been permitted to attend performances at half price. The Kennedy Center is dependent on box-office revenues and private gifts to carry out its congressional mandate, not only in respect to the performing arts but in respect to public-service programming as well; during 1980, a total of well over three million dollars was raised from corporations, foundations, and individuals. The Center is open every day of the year and the average occupancy rate of its auditoriums has been eighty per cent—probably the highest rate of any cultural enterprise in the country.

A more subtle measure of the Center's success is the degree to which it has entered the consciousness of the entire country. As a memorial to President Kennedy and as what he foresaw and labored to bring into being—a worthy place in which to display the country's highest aspirations in the performing arts—the Center has become one of the three most popular sites in the capital. Grandiose as the building itself seems at first glance, tourists feel at home there. They stroll about the great halls or up and down the immense salon in the conventional undress of travellers, with cameras and kit bags slung over their shoulders and often enough with a baby in arms. They are impressed by the Center but not awed by it; plainly, they do not find its multiplicity of programs intimidating. They are at ease with the notion that this palace of marble and glass exists for their entertainment and education; in a profound sense, it belongs to them and they do well to be happy there.

Ten years have passed since Roger L. Stevens stood on the stage of the Opera House and spoke the first words of welcome at the ceremonies that served to open the Center. Twenty years have passed since he accepted President Kennedy's invitation to become chairman of an institution that then consisted entirely of paper—a printed statute and an armful of architectural drawings. Few men have had the opportunity to turn a risky dream into a flourishing reality; Stevens has been quoted as saying that he finds it harder to run a cultural center than it was to build one, but he smiles as he utters the complaint. It is evident that his appetite for difficulties remains undiminished. His physical appearance has changed astonishingly little over the years; if, after two heart attacks and a recent triple heart-bypass operation, he is under doctors' orders to husband his energies, he continues to be a hard man to keep up with. Planes to him are a species of taxi; one day he is in Washington, the next in Seattle, New York, or Paris. In a single week in the early summer of 1981, he gave a talk before a gathering of museum directors in Florence, flew on to Salzburg to address some theatre people attending a session of the Salzburg Seminar in American Studies, and then, finding that he had a free day before his next appointment, which was in London, hastened on to the South of France, to pass a night there with old friends. Meanwhile, he was keeping in touch daily by telephone with his offices in Washington and New York.

Any anniversary is an occasion, if one chooses to seize it, for summing up and perhaps also for announcing changes of direction on the part of an institution or an individual. If Stevens has such changes in mind concerning his personal future, he has yet to speak of them; close friends assume that he will continue working, because they cannot imagine him doing otherwise. In the words of Richard Cumberland, his aspiration is to wear out, not rust out; as one of his associates has said, "Roger has no talent for idleness. Just to think about his trying it makes me nervous." For the Center, Stevens has plans as well as hopes. Additional garage space is urgently needed; a new building could be put up partly for that practical purpose and partly for a purpose much closer to Stevens' heart—the housing of a conservatory of music and theatre, to which students would come from all over the country. "I've all but promised it to Rostropovich [director of the National Symphony] if all the problems can be solved," Stevens has said, "and I'm a man who likes to keep his promises. More money to raise! Once in a while, I find myself wondering where I'll find the energy to go out and raise it, but the doubt passes. Somehow or other, if the cause is good enough, the money turns up." Stevens' candid blue eyes gleamed with amusement. "There's an irony implicit in anything that succeeds," he said. "From the vantage point of success, it looks as if it couldn't possibly have failed. So with the Center. Twenty years ago, there were any number of people here in Washington eager to tell us that the Center wouldn't work—that even if we could manage to get it built, it would stand idle most of the time. At the moment, the doomsayers are silent, but they haven't gone away. Maybe I'll get a chance to rouse them one more time."

KENNEDY CENTER
IN COLOR

Though a Southern city, Washington can know severe winter weather. The formidable bulk of the Center is agreeably reduced by the presence of snow. After ten years, the land surrounding the Center is beginning to assume the parklike look that existed at first only in architectural renderings of the site. As the trees and other plantings grow, the Center seems to settle more and more comfortably into place above the riverbank. In the foreground is Spain's gift to the Center—a sculpture in bronze and stone entitled "Don Quixote."

At left and below:
The Center as decorated
in honor of the arrival
of the Vienna State Opera.

Above: In the Hall of Nations hang the flags of
all the nations with which the United States
currently maintains diplomatic relations.
The total is one hundred and thirty-nine;
surprisingly, there is room for a few more flags.

Overleaf: Constellations of fireworks hang in
the sky above the Center on the Fourth of July.

57

The photographer Yoichi Okamoto has long
been preoccupied with lights reflected in
window glass and on other polished surfaces.
The eighteen crystal chandeliers that illuminate
the Grand Foyer were a gift from Sweden.

At left: Stevens photographed in the Grand Foyer. In the background rises the colossal bronze head of John F. Kennedy, by the sculptor Robert Berks. At right: The staff of the Center, looking very much as if they were posing for a happy-go-lucky high-school graduation photograph.

Night and day, the open spaces that surround the Center accommodate themselves with equal ease to large, formally dressed audiences and to small groups of passing tourists.

Overleaf: From the upper terrace, visitors look out in all directions over the city and its curving ribbon of river. Long ago, Washington chose not to scrape the sky with commercial buildings; the Washington Monument and the Capitol, not only in their nature as symbols but in their physical measurements as well, remain the city's loftiest presences.

Before the Grand Foyer was built, many people feared that it would be too big to justify itself in practical terms; on the contrary, it has proved to be both practical and popular. It serves as a lobby for the three main auditoriums of the Center and as a successful auditorium in its own right. Moreover, it is one of the few spaces in the city able to shelter the vast crowds attendant upon the inauguration of a President. Benefits and other social events make constant use of one or another of the Center's multiple facilities. In a short lifetime, it has become an indispensable part of the public life of Washington.

Overleaf: In a bedazzlement of lights, audiences mingle in the Grand Foyer, providing a source of entertainment in themselves as they while away an intermission with drinks and animated conversation.

*A concert may last only a couple of hours, but
behind the concert lie many hours of rehearsals,
which consist in part of drudgery and in part
of the tedium of waiting for others.*

Reflections in a golden trumpet.

Itzhak Perlman and Isaac Stern, two much-favored performers at the Center.

Upper left: Mstislav Rostropovich conducting the National Symphony.
Like many other conductors, including Toscanini, it appears that he sings at his work.

Lower left: Leonard Slatkin, conducting the Mostly Mozart Festival Orchestra during the
Center's first "Festival of Festivals," in the early summer of 1981.

Overleaf: The Concert Hall as viewed from its ample upper tier.

Sometimes the public is invited to attend rehearsals. Schoolchildren are among the most avid of listeners, and all the more so when they may sit at their ease and perhaps dispense altogether with chairs. The concertgoer at the left appears to have arrived somewhat earlier than was absolutely necessary.

Instruments available to performers at the Center include the Filene Organ with four thousand pipes (the gift of former trustee Mrs. Jouett Shouse) and an antique harpsichord.

Below: A view of the Concert Hall from the vantage point of a patient tympanist.

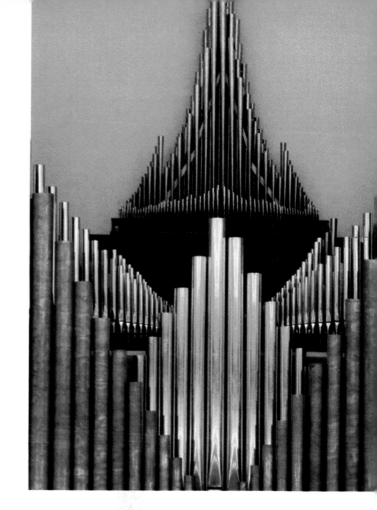

More than four thousand performances have been given in the Eisenhower Theater.
Three plays by Preston Jones, bearing the common title "A Texas Trilogy," have been
among the longest-running. In one of them—"The Oldest Living Graduate"—
Fred Gwynne played a noisy old rascal in a wheelchair.

Lower left: Stagehands at work on a set that requires the use of a turntable.

The Terrace Theater is a gift of the government and the people of Japan to the people of the United States, in commemoration of the American Bicentennial. It was designed by Philip Johnson and John Burgee. Shown are scenes from a performance of the Grand Kabuki, on a visit to Washington from Tokyo to dedicate the Terrace Theater.

Aaron Copland being greeted by Martin Feinstein, General Director of The Washington Opera and formerly the Center's Executive Director for Performing Arts.
Left below: Two loyal supporters of the Center — Henry Strong, whose father, L. Corrin Strong, provided the first funding for the Center, and Patrick Hayes, a veteran Washington impresario.
In 1978, an annual event entitled "Kennedy Center Honors: A National Celebration of the Arts" was inaugurated at the Center and broadcast coast-to-coast by CBS-TV. Five persons are chosen each year by the Board of Trustees of the Center. In 1978, the honors list included Marian Anderson, Fred Astaire, George Balanchine, Richard Rodgers, and Arthur Rubinstein. At right above: Fred Astaire being toasted by Mrs. Polk Guest and Gregory Peck. At right: Alberta Hunter is among the performers providing entertainment. At far right: Marian Anderson with her dinner companion Michael Sweeley, Director of the Caramoor Festival.

In 1979, the Kennedy Honors List included
Aaron Copland, Ella Fitzgerald, Henry Fonda,
Martha Graham, and Tennessee Williams.

Far left above: The bemedaled Mr. Fonda
chats with Alan Alda and his wife.

Far left below: Tennessee Williams.

At left: Lillian Gish and Miss Graham.

Below: Count Basie making merry.

A scene from a charming little musical called "Tintypes" was one of the star turns of the Honors evening in 1980.

90

The artists honored in 1980, from left to right:
Leonard Bernstein, Agnes de Mille, Leontyne Price,
James Cagney, and Lynn Fontanne.

Leonard Bernstein's "Mass, a Theatre Piece for Singers, Players, and Dancers" inaugurated the Kennedy Center when it was given its premiere in the Opera House on September 8, 1971. Alan Titus sang the role of Celebrant. Bernstein was among those who were awarded Kennedy Center Honors in 1980. His "Mass" was also performed at the Center as part of the September, 1981, Anniversary Celebration.

93

To be successful, the design and decoration
of an opera house should partake of fantasy
and melodrama. The Center's Opera House
achieves its effects in large measure by
means of the brilliance of its lighting; the
chandelier was the gift of Austria.
At right: Timothy Nolen in Carlisle Floyd's
"Willie Stark," an opera commissioned by the
Kennedy Center and co-produced with the
Houston Grand Opera.

Overleaf: The opera company Teatro alla
Scala, of Milan, paid its first visit to America
in 1976 to perform Verdi's "Macbeth" at
the Center as one of the highlights of our
Bicentennial celebrations.

The Peking Opera visited the Center in
1980. A glimpse of dancers backstage.

Far left: The Vienna State Opera made its
first appearance in America when it gave
a much-admired performance of Beethoven's
"Fidelio" in the Opera House.

At left: The Paris Opera presented three
operas during its historic 1976 appearance,
including Mozart's "Le Nozze di Figaro,"
featuring Edith Mathis.

Renata Scotto in Puccini's "Manon Lescaut," given during the Metropolitan Opera's engagement at the Center in 1981.

Right above: In 1975, the Houston Grand Opera brought to the Opera House Scott Joplin's "Treemonisha," starring Carmen Balthrop.

Right below: Beverly Sills made her farewell appearance at the Center on May 5, 1979, in a New York City Opera production of Rossini's "The Turk in Italy." (She is flanked onstage, from left to right, by Martin Feinstein, Roger L. Stevens, and Julius Rudel.)

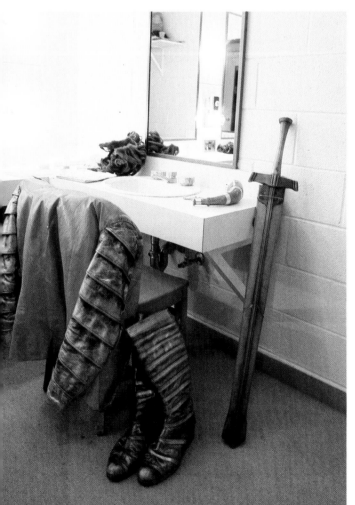

Handel's opera "Ariodante" was staged for the first time in America during the opening week of the Center. It starred Beverly Sills, Tatiana Troyanos, and Donald Gramm.

Left above: A scene from Verdi's "Un Ballo in Maschera," given by the Washington Opera on the twenty-fifth anniversary of its founding.

Left below: Mussorgsky's "Boris Godunov" in a production by the Bolshoi Opera.

At left: Much effort goes into creating an illusion onstage; no illusions are to be expected backstage, where props often consort oddly with plumbing.

Overleaf: A scene from the Bolshoi Opera's production of Prokofiev's "War and Peace."

103

Right above: In 1980, the World Puppetry Festival, held for the first time in the United States at the Kennedy Center, cooperated with the Education Program of the Center to offer free performances for children.

Right below: A scene from Wendy Kesselman's play "Maggie Magalita," commissioned for the annual National Children's Arts Festival, the Imagination Celebration, 1980.

Below: A performance of Goldoni's "The Servant of Two Masters," given during the American College Theatre Festival, in 1974, by the University of Wisconsin at Milwaukee.

Roger L. Stevens discusses an upcoming production in the Theater Lab.

At right: Before a performance, dressing rooms can be among the tensest places on earth; later, there is time for relaxation. Stevens and Jane Alexander chat after the curtain has fallen on "The First Monday in October," a play by Jerome Lawrence and Robert E. Lee, starring Henry Fonda and Miss Alexander, which opened at the Eisenhower Theater before going on to New York for a successful run. Thanks to a sufficiency of mirrors, we see two Stevenses and three Alexanders.

At right: Among the most popular musical comedies to play in the Opera House has been "Fiddler on the Roof," starring Zero Mostel. Below: "Barnum," starring Stacy Keach, and far right, "The Pajama Game," starring Barbara McNair. Far right below: Also a big hit was the D'Oyly Carte production of Gilbert and Sullivan's "H.M.S. Pinafore."

Four stars in a revival of "The Royal Family" by George S. Kaufman and Edna Ferber. From left to right, Eva Le Gallienne, Sam Levene, Rosemary Harris, and George Grizzard.

Right above: Deborah Kerr and Monty Markham in "The Last of Mrs. Cheyney" by Frederick Lonsdale.

Right below: Constance Cummings in Arthur Kopit's "Wings."

Far left above: A much-praised production of Eugene O'Neill's "Long Day's Journey into Night," with Jason Robards, Jr., Zoe Caldwell, Michael Moriarty, and Kevin Conway. Far left below: Anthony Quayle and Mary Martin in a comedy by the Russian dramatist Aleksei Arbuzov, "Do You Turn Somersaults?" On this page, above: Irene Worth and Christopher Walken played in Tennessee Williams' "Sweet Bird of Youth" during the American Bicentennial Theatre Season produced by the Kennedy Center. Below: The musical "Annie" by Thomas Meehan, Charles Strouse, and Martin Charnin.

The Theater Lab is, as its name implies, an experimental theatre space operated by the Center. At top: A scene from Robert Wilson's production of "Medea." Above: A scene from "The Invasion of Addis Ababa" by James Bronson, which was given a reading under the auspices of the Center's Black Theatre and Playwright Project. At right: Angela Lansbury and George Hearn as happy accomplices in murder in Stephen Sondheim's "Sweeney Todd."

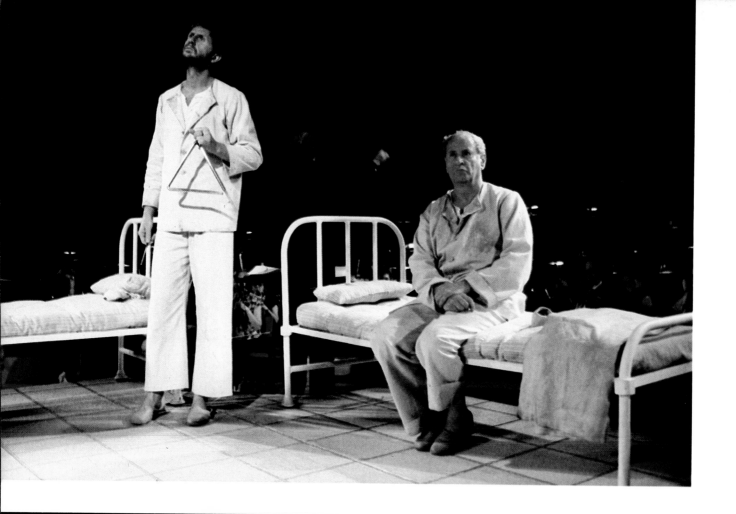

Above: Wilfrid Hyde-White being benignly clerical in a scene from "The Prodigal Daughter" by David Turner. His companions are John Lithgow and Stephen Elliot.

Far left above: Eli Wallach and René Auberjonois in "Every Good Boy Deserves Favour" by Tom Stoppard. Far left below: A scene from "The Mighty Gents" by Richard Wesley.

Left: Lilli Palmer in a one-woman show about the "divine" Sarah Bernhardt. Miss Palmer gave the show first in the Eisenhower Theater and then on public television in "Kennedy Center Tonight!"

119

TICKETS

The Kennedy Center box office is accustomed to welcoming a variety of visitors in a variety of conveyances. Right above: The Stuttgart Ballet dances "The Sleeping Beauty" in a production directed by Rosella Hightower. Right below: The Royal Ballet performs "Swan Lake."

Natalia Makarova made an early appearance at the Center in "Shakespeare: Dance and Drama," successfully inaugurating the Center's third season.

Far left above: Baryshnikov dancing in "Don Quixote" with the American Ballet Theatre. Far left below: The American Ballet Theatre production of "The Nutcracker." Each of these productions had its world premiere in the Opera House.

The Dance Theater of Harlem
performing "Serenade."

At right: Suzanne Farrell and
Peter Martins of the New York
City Ballet, in "Jewels."

Far right: The Martha Graham
Dance Company in "Frescoes."

Overleaf: The Center finds room from time to time for exhibitions having to do with the performing arts. This one, funded by International Business Machines, celebrated two hundred years of performing arts under the title "America on Stage."

Far left: The Israeli Room is an attractive place in which to entertain distinguished visitors to the Center. Below: Similarly attractive is the African Room, the gift of twenty-two African nations.

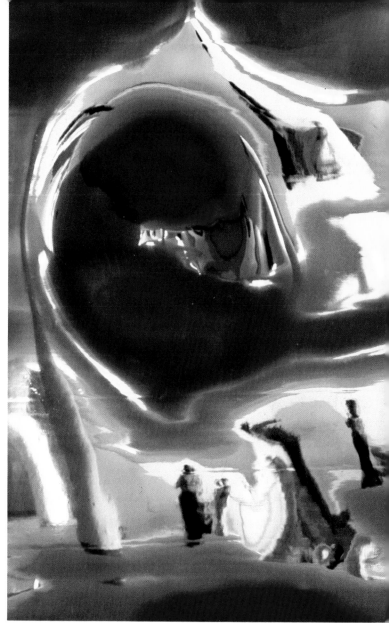

Willy Weber's sculpture "Apollo Ten, 1970" may be seen in the lobby of the Concert Hall.

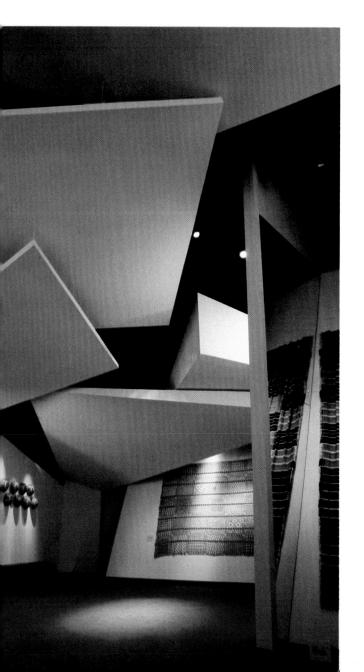

129

The most recent accomplishment of the Center is the Performing Arts
Library, for which ample room was found on the top floor of the
Center. It is a joint undertaking with the Library of Congress, much
of whose incomparable resources are instantly available to the
Performing Arts Library by means of video computers.

Left above: The American Film Institute Theatre, which was
ingeniously fitted into some unused backstage space at the Eisenhower
Theater. Left below: Members of the organization known as Friends
of the Kennedy Center serve as volunteer guides, taking thousands of
visitors through the Center on every day of the year.

On the evening of September 12, 1981, the tenth anniversary of the opening of the Center was celebrated by a party for which, according to custom, a birthday cake provided the climax. Below: The cake, a reasonably accurate confectionary facsimile of the Center, is being partitioned with grave care by Roger L. Stevens, as Senator Charles H. Percy, a trustee of the Center, and John Bookout, President of the Shell Oil Company, look on, and a caterer prepares to distribute pieces of the cake to guests. At left: Enjoying the cake are Mrs. Henry Strong, former Senator J. William Fulbright (one of the two original sponsors of the legislation that brought the Center into existence), and Henry Strong, trustee.

PROGRAMMING HIGHLIGHTS OF THE JOHN F. KENNEDY CENTER

1971–1981

OPERA HOUSE

1971–1972 Season

MASS (September 8–9, 16–19, 1971)

The world premiere of Leonard Bernstein's "Mass, a Theatre Piece for Singers, Players, and Dancers," created especially for the dedication of the John F. Kennedy Center for the Performing Arts, officially opened the Opera House on Wednesday, September 8. Alan Titus and Walter Willison sang the role of Celebrant; the cast also included the Norman Scribner Choir, the Berkshire Boys' Choir, and the Alvin Ailey American Dance Theatre. Bernstein based his work on the liturgy of the Roman Mass, incorporating additional English texts by himself and Stephen Schwartz.

BEATRIX CENCI (September 10, 12, and 13, 1971)

The world premiere of Alberto Ginastera's opera was the first in a series of operas presented by the Opera Society of Washington, a resident affiliate of Kennedy Center. The title role was sung by American soprano Arlene Saunders, and Justino Diaz played the role of the villain Count. "Beatrix Cenci" was conducted by the Center's first Music Director, Julius Rudel.

ARIODANTE (September 14 and 16, 1971)

Handel's opera was staged for the first time in America. Presented by the Center as part of its two-week festival of music and dance inaugurating the Center's theatres, it was conducted by Julius Rudel and starred Beverly Sills, Tatiana Troyanos, and Donald Gramm.

AMERICAN BALLET THEATRE (September 11, 15, 21–October 3, 1971)

The official ballet company of the John F. Kennedy Center opened its two-week inaugural engagement with its full-length production of "Swan Lake" after two special performances for the Gala opening week. During its 1971–72 inaugural season at Kennedy Center, the American Ballet Theatre presented more than three dozen ballets, including full-length productions of "Giselle," "Swan Lake," and "Les Sylphides."

The American Ballet Theatre has been presented annually at the Center since 1971 in twenty appearances. Mikhail Baryshnikov's "The Nutcracker," "Don Quixote," and "Raymonda Divertissements" (1976, 1978, 1980), and Anthony Tudor's "The Tiller in the Fields" (1976) have had their world premieres at Kennedy Center.

CANDIDE (October 26–November 14, 1971)

Leonard Bernstein's new production of his musical, based on the satire by Voltaire, featured Frank Porretta, Mary Costa, Rae Allen, and Robert Klein. Director and book adaptation, Sheldon Patinkin, Musical Director, Maurice Peress, and lyrics provided by Richard Wilbur.

AFRO-ASIAN DANCE FESTIVAL (November 15–21, 1971)

The Washington Performing Arts Society, a Center affiliate, sponsored an Afro-Asian Dance Festival as a tribute to the inauguration of the

Julius Rudel discussing Handel's opera "Ariodante" with Tatiana Troyanos and Veronica Tyler.

Center. The Festival featured four troupes never before seen in the United States: The Senegalese National Dance Company; The Zour Khaneh Ceremonial Athletes of Iran; the Classical Khmer Dancers of Cambodia; and The National Dance Company of Morocco.

FALSTAFF *(December 2–3, 5–6, 1971, part of a series)*

Verdi's opera under the sponsorship of the Opera Society of Washington starred Robert Savoie in his American operatic stage debut.

NEW YORK CITY OPERA *(April 3–14, 1972)*

First appearance at Kennedy Center featured Donizetti's "Roberto Devereux" and Janáček's "The Makropoulos Affair." The Company made annual appearances through 1979.

A VILLAGE ROMEO AND JULIET *(April 26, 27, and 28, 1972)*

The American premiere of Delius's opera, under the sponsorship of the Opera Society of Washington, starred John Stewart and Patricia Wells.

1972–1973 *Season*

FESTIVAL OF THE OLD AND THE NEW *(September 4–9, 1972)*

The Kennedy Center inaugurated its second season with a performance of Cimarosa's "Il Matrimonio Segreto," a two-act opera presented by the Rome Piccolo Opera, as part of the Festival of the Old and the New. The Rome Piccolo Opera also performed Paisiello's "Barbiere di Siviglia," and Vivaldi's dramatic oratorio, "Juditha Triumphans." Soloists from Milan's La Scala and the Rome Opera were featured.

PIPPIN *(September 20–October 4, 1972)*

World premiere, directed by Bob Fosse, produced by Stuart Ostrow, with music and lyrics by Stephen Schwartz, book by Roger O. Hirson. John Rubenstein starred in the title role; Jill Clayburgh, Ben Vereen, Irene Ryan, Leland Palmer, and Eric Berry also appeared.

THE LAST OF MRS. LINCOLN *(November 13–December 2, 1972)*

Premiere of James Prideaux's drama starred Julie Harris in the role of Mrs. Lincoln.

THE RISE AND FALL OF THE CITY OF MAHAGONNY *(December 15, 17–19, 1972)*

Bertolt Brecht-Kurt Weill's opera was presented by the Opera Society of Washington.

EMPEROR HENRY IV *(March 5–24, 1973)*

Luigi Pirandello's play starred Rex Harrison.

STUTTGART BALLET *(June 5–17, 1973)*

The Stuttgart Ballet, presented by the Kennedy Center, staged its first appearance at the Center, featuring prima ballerina Marcia Haydee. Two full-length ballets were performed, "Romeo and Juliet" and "Swan Lake," along with performances of three new works by John Cranko, then Director of the Stuttgart Ballet.

The Stuttgart Ballet returned in 1977 and 1979, during the latter engagement presenting the American premiere of John Neumeier's "Lady of the Camellias" as part of the festival, Paris: The Romantic Epoch.

1973–1974 *Season*

SHAKESPEARE: DANCE AND DRAMA
(September 25–30, 1973)

A program of ballet and theatre was featured as part of the festival devoted to Shakespeare and the Performing Arts, which inaugurated the third season at Kennedy Center. Maurice Evans, Kathleen Widdoes, Dame Peggy Ashcroft, Michael Redgrave, Natalia Makarova, Cynthia Gregory, and Ivan Nagy were principal performers.

A STREETCAR NAMED DESIRE
(November 20–25, 1973)

Tennessee Williams's Pulitzer Prize-winning play starred Lois Nettleton and Alan Feinstein.

Rex Harrison in Pirandello's "Emperor Henry IV."

Ben Vereen and his harlequin troupe in "Pippin."

NEW YORK CITY BALLET
(February 19–March 3, 1974)

The New York City Ballet made its first appearance at the Kennedy Center. The opening engagement was launched with George Balanchine's full-length version of Shakespeare's "A Midsummer Night's Dream," starring Kay Mazzo. Three Washington premieres were also presented: "Four Bagatelles," "Variations pour une Porte et un Soupir," and Tchaikovsky's Suite No. 3. The Company has been presented annually through the 1980–1981 season.

SHOWBOAT *(May 7–19, 1974)*

The Jerome Kern-Oscar Hammerstein musical starred Mickey Rooney, Linda Michele, Jerry Lanning, and Leonard Hayward.

MOZART FESTIVAL *(May 23–26, 1974)*

As part of the Mozart Festival, the opera "Idomeneo" was conducted by the Center's Music Director, Julius Rudel, starring Richard Taylor, Leo Goeke, Maralin Niska, and Elly Ameling.

Also as part of the Mozart Festival, three performances were staged of the New York City Opera production of "Le Nozze di Figaro," starring Robert Hale, Gwenlynn Little, Maria Ewing, and Johanna Meier, conducted by Charles Wendelken-Wilson and the Center's Music Director, Julius Rudel.

ROYAL BALLET (*May 28–June 9, 1974*)

London's famed Royal Ballet made its premiere appearance with a two-week engagement. The repertory included Frederick Ashton's "La Fille Mal Gardée," Petipa's "La Bayadère," Kenneth MacMillan's "Manon," "Romeo and Juliet" and "Swan Lake." The Royal Ballet returned in 1976 and again in 1981.

GYPSY (*August 13–31, 1974*)

Angela Lansbury starred in the musical based on the memoirs of stripper Gypsy Rose Lee, written by Arthur Laurents (book), Jule Styne (music), and Stephen Sondheim (lyrics).

1974–1975 Season

L'INCORONAZIONE DI POPPEA
(*October 9–13, 1974*)

As part of the Kennedy Center's Venetian Festival, the Opera Society of Washington staged Monteverdi's opera, starring Noel Rogers and Alan Titus.

Ingrid Bergman in "The Constant Wife" by W. Somerset Maugham.

IN PRAISE OF LOVE
(*November 12–30, 1974*)

Terence Rattigan's play starred Rex Harrison, Julie Harris, and Martin Gabel.

CAT ON A HOT TIN ROOF
(*February 12–March 1, 1975*)

Tennessee Williams's play starred Elizabeth Ashley, Fred Gwynne, along with Michael Zaslow and Kate Reid.

THE CONSTANT WIFE (*March 4–22, 1975*)

W. Somerset Maugham's comedy starred Ingrid Bergman.

PEARL BAILEY IN CONCERT
(*April 7–13, 1975*)

BOLSHOI BALLET (*May 27–June 1, 1975*)

As part of the Kennedy Center's Bicentennial Celebration, a Gala Benefit presented Russia's Bolshoi Ballet with the three-act ballet "Spartacus," starring Vladimir Vasiliev, Maris Liepa, Nina Sorokina, and Nina Timofeyeva, marking the Bolshoi Ballet's first appearance in the United States in more than a decade. During the Company's one-week engagement it performed three full-length ballets: "Ivan the Terrible," Grigorovich's newest ballet, and "Giselle" as well as "Spartacus."

BOLSHOI OPERA (*July 22–August 3, 1975*)

As part of the Kennedy Center's Bicentennial Celebration, Russia's Bolshoi Opera made its United States premiere with a two-week engagement—the largest ensemble to have performed on the Center's stage to date. The Company opened with Mussorgsky's "Boris Godunov," starring Yevgeni Nesterenko as Boris. Four additional operas performed were: Tchaikovsky's "Eugene Onegin" and "Pique Dame" ("The Queen of Spades"), and Sergei Prokofiev's "War and Peace" and "The Gambler." The operas performed were five of its most famous productions.

Ekaterina Maximova and Mikhail Lavrovsky in the Bolshoi Ballet's "Spartacus."

Mako starred in the musical "Pacific Overtures."

1975–1976 Season

TREEMONISHA *(September 3–21, 1975)*

The Houston Grand Opera's production of Scott Joplin's opera starred Carmen Balthrop, Curtis Rayam, and Betty Allen.

BERLIN OPERA *(November 14–29, 1975)*

As a tribute to the Center's Bicentennial Celebration, the Berlin Opera made its American debut with the performance of Wagner's "Lohengrin," conducted by Lorin Maazel. During the company's two-week engagement, Puccini's "Tosca" and Mozart's "Cosi Fan Tutte" were also performed under the direction of Lorin Maazel and Karl Böhm respectively.

PACIFIC OVERTURES
(December 4–27, 1975)

The Harold Prince-Stephen Sondheim musical starred Mako and Soon-Teck Oh, with Yuki Shimoda.

HELLO, DOLLY!
(December 30, 1975–January 24, 1976)

The farewell appearance of Pearl Bailey in "Hello, Dolly!"

BICENTENNIAL SALUTE TO THE PERFORMING ARTS
GALA HONORING ROGER L. STEVENS
(January 25, 1976)

Henry Fonda hosted the Kennedy Center's Bicentennial Salute to the Performing Arts, honoring the Center's Chairman, Roger L. Stevens. The spectacular evening of entertainment featured Carol Channing, Isaac Stern, lyricists Betty Comden and Adolph Green, and many others. Two scenes were shown from the smash hit, "A Chorus Line."

ROYAL DANISH BALLET *(May 11–16, 1976)*

As Denmark's Salute to the American Bicentennial, the Royal Danish Ballet premiered with two Bournonville ballets, "Guards of Amager," never before seen in the United States, and the third act of "Napoli," as well as Roland Petit's "Carmen." Other ballets performed during their engagement included "The Four Seasons" and "The Triumph of Death."

FIDDLER ON THE ROOF
(July 13–August 7, 1976)

Zero Mostel starred in the musical by Jerry Bock, Sheldon Harnick, and Joseph Stein.

1976–1977 Season

TEATRO ALLA SCALA
(September 7–19, 1976)

As a major highlight of the Center's Bicentennial Celebration, Teatro alla Scala made its first appearance in the United States with an exclusive two-week engagement at the Kennedy Center, with Verdi's "Macbeth," starring mezzo-soprano Shirley Verrett. Puccini's "La Bohème," Rossini's "La Cenerentola," and Verdi's "Simon Boccanegra" were also presented.

PARIS OPERA *(September 21–October 3, 1976)*

As an operatic salute to the Center's Bicentennial Celebration, the Paris Opera presented Verdi's "Otello." During the Company's Washington, D.C. engagement, two additional operas were performed—"Le Nozze di Figaro" and "Faust."

AMERICAN BALLET THEATRE
(December 21, 1976–January 2, 1977)

World premiere performance of the Tchaikovsky ballet "The Nutcracker," choreographed and directed by Mikhail Baryshnikov.

CAESAR AND CLEOPATRA
(January 10–29, 1977)

George Bernard Shaw's play starred Rex Harrison and Elizabeth Ashley.

PRE-INAUGURAL GALA *(January 19, 1977)*

The Pre-Inaugural Gala honored President-elect Jimmy Carter and Mrs. Carter.

PORGY AND BESS *(July 13–31, 1977)*

The 1977 Tony Award-winning Houston Grand Opera production of "Porgy and Bess," George Gershwin's masterpiece.

1977–1978 Season

A CHORUS LINE
(September 15–November 5, 1977)

The musical by Marvin Hamlisch, Edward Klebau, James Kirkwood, and Nicholas Dante.

Gershwin's masterpiece "Porgy and Bess" with Donnie Ray Albert and Wilhelmenia Fernandez.

TIMBUKTU *(January 14–February 5, 1978)*

With music and lyrics by Robert Wright and George Forrest, it starred Eartha Kitt, Melba Moore, William Marshall, and Gilbert Price.

THE SEAGULL *(February 8–12, 1978)*

The American premiere of Thomas Pasatieri's opera was presented by the Washington Opera.

ALVIN AILEY AMERICAN DANCE THEATRE *(February 14–19, 1978)*

D'OYLY CARTE OPERA *(April 3–29, 1978)*

The D'Oyly Carte Opera performed Gilbert and Sullivan's "Iolanthe," "Pinafore," "Mikado," "Princess Ida," and "The Pirates of Penzance."

BALLET NACIONAL DE CUBA
(May 30–June 11, 1978)

The first U.S. appearance of the Ballet featured prima ballerina Alicia Alonso.

THE WIZ (*June 15–July 29, 1978*)

With music and lyrics by Charlie Smalls, book by William F. Brown.

1978–1979 *Season*

PLATINUM (*September 30–October 28, 1978*)

"Platinum" by Gary Friedman, Will Holt, and Bruce Vilavek, starred Alexis Smith.

THE FIRST KENNEDY CENTER HONORS GALA (*December 3, 1978*)

The first such Gala honored the achievements of Fred Astaire, George Balanchine, Marian Anderson, Richard Rodgers, and Arthur Rubinstein.

AMERICA ENTERTAINS VICE-PREMIER DENG XIAOPING (*January 29, 1979*)

Vice-Premier Deng Xiaoping was entertained in a program sponsored by the National Council for U.S.-China Trade, featuring the Broadway company of "Eubie," Rudolf Serkin, and the Joffrey Ballet.

GRAND KABUKI OF JAPAN (*January 30–February 4, 1979*)

CARMELINA (*March 7–24, 1979*)

By Joseph Stein, Alan Jay Lerner, and Burton Lane, it starred Georgia Brown and Cesare Siepi.

NEW YORK CITY OPERA (*May 1–13, 1979*)

Rossini's "The Turk in Italy," with Beverly Sills in her final gala Washington appearance.

PETER PAN (*July 17–August 5, 1979*)

"Peter Pan" by Mark Charlap, Carolyn Leigh, Betty Comden, and Adolph Green, starred Sandy Duncan and George Rose.

OKLAHOMA (*August 8–September 9, 1979*)

The revival of Rodgers and Hammerstein's musical with Lawrence Guittard, Christine Andreas, and Mary Wickes.

Eartha Kitt (right) and George Bell in "Timbuktu."

"Peter Pan" with Sandy Duncan and Marsha Kramer.

1979–1980 Season

CENDRILLON (September 15–21, 23, 1979)

The Washington Opera presented Jules Massenet's "Cendrillon," starring Frederica Von Stade.

VIENNA STATE OPERA
(October 27–November 11, 1979)

The first appearance in America of the Vienna State Opera featured Beethoven's "Fidelio," conducted by Leonard Bernstein; Strauss's "Salome," conducted by Zubin Mehta; Mozart's "Le Nozze di Figaro," conducted by Karl Böhm; and Strauss's "Ariadne auf Naxos," conducted by Karl Böhm.

LIZA MINNELLI (November 13–18, 1979)

THE SECOND KENNEDY CENTER HONORS GALA (December 2, 1979)

The second Gala honored Aaron Copland, Ella Fitzgerald, Henry Fonda, Martha Graham, and Tennessee Williams.

WEST SIDE STORY
(January 4–February 3, 1980)

The first major revival of the landmark musical by Arthur Laurents, Leonard Bernstein, and Stephen Sondheim, restaged by Jerome Robbins.

WASHINGTON OPERA BENEFIT RECITAL BY BIRGIT NILSSON
(Feb. 26, 1980)

METROPOLITAN OPERA
(April 21–26, 1980)

Under the direction of James Levine, first appearance at the Kennedy Center Opera House, opening with Luciano Pavarotti in Donizetti's "L'Elisir d'Amore." The Met returned in 1981 for a two-week engagement featuring six productions and the Verdi Requiem.

SHANGHAI ACROBATIC THEATRE FROM THE PEOPLE'S REPUBLIC OF CHINA (April 29–May 4, 1980)

The first American appearance.

42ND STREET (June 22–July 27, 1980)

Directed and choreographed by the late Gower Champion, it starred Tammy Grimes and Jerry Ohrbach.

BERLIN OPERA BALLET
(July 20–August 10, 1980)

The Washington debut of the Berlin Opera Ballet premiered "The Idiot," choreographed and danced by Valery Panov, and "The Nutcracker," choreographed by Rudolph Nureyev.

1980-1981 Season

PEKING OPERA *(September 2-14, 1980)*

The first Washington appearance of the Peking Opera offered "Monkey King Fights 18 Lo Hans."

WASHINGTON OPERA TWENTY-FIFTH ANNIVERSARY *(September 20, 1980)*

Presenting Verdi's "Un Ballo in Maschera."

NEW YORK CITY BALLET
(October 8-19, 1980)

Featuring the Washington premiere of George Balanchine's "Robert Schumann's Davidsbündlertänze."

SWEENEY TODD
(October 26-November 29, 1980)

The Stephen Sondheim musical starred Angela Lansbury and George Hearn.

THE THIRD KENNEDY CENTER HONORS GALA *(December 7, 1980)*

The third Gala honored Agnes de Mille, James Cagney, Leonard Bernstein, Lynn Fontanne, and Leontyne Price.

AMERICAN BALLET THEATRE
(December 10-21, 1980)

The first Kennedy Center engagement under the artistic directorship of Mikhail Baryshnikov featured the Washington premiere of Natalia Makarova's "La Bayadère" and the world premiere of "Raymonda" (Divertissements from Acts II and III), staged by Mikhail Baryshnikov.

PRE-INAUGURAL GALA CONCERT
(January 18, 1981)

The Pre-Inaugural Gala honoring President-elect Ronald Reagan and Mrs. Reagan featured stars from the opera and ballet.

DANCE THEATER OF HARLEM
(February 10-15, 1981)

It featured its new production of "Scheherazade," sponsored by the Washington Performing Arts Society, as part of the first Dance America Series.

ELIOT FELD BALLET
(February 17-22, 1981)

Jointly sponsored by the Center and the Washington Performing Arts Society, as part of the first Dance America Series, the Eliot Feld Ballet included Washington premieres of "Circa" and "Meadowlark."

MARTHA GRAHAM DANCE COMPANY
(February 24-March 1, 1981)

Under the joint sponsorship of the Center and the Washington Performing Arts Society, as part of the first Dance America Series, the company presented the world premiere of "Acts of Light."

WILLIE STARK *(May 9-29, 1981)*

Carlisle Floyd's musical drama, based on Robert Penn Warren's *All the King's Men*, was commissioned by the Kennedy Center, produced jointly with the Houston Grand Opera, and featured Timothy Nolen as the Southern politician.

ROYAL BALLET *(July 14-26, 1981)*

In its fiftieth anniversary season, Britain's famed Royal Ballet presented Washington premieres of Frederick Ashton's "Daphnis and Chloe" and Kenneth MacMillan's "Gloria" and "Isadora."

ANNIE *(July 31-September 5, 1981)*

The award-winning musical by Thomas Meehan, Charles Strouse, and Martin Charnin returned to Kennedy Center where it had originated in 1977 in the Eisenhower Theater.

EISENHOWER THEATER

1971–1972 Season

A DOLL'S HOUSE
(October 18–November 6, 1971)

The Hillard Elkins production of Henrik Ibsen's classic opened the new Eisenhower Theater, starring Claire Bloom and Ed Zimmermann.

A COUNTRY GIRL
(November 16–December 18, 1971)

As part of the inaugural season of the John F. Kennedy Center, Clifford Odets' drama starred Jason Robards, Jr., Maureen Stapleton, and George Grizzard.

THE TIME OF YOUR LIFE
(January 15–February 5, 1972)

William Saroyan's Pulitzer Prize-winning play opened its national tour, starring Henry Fonda. Co-starring were Jane Alexander, Richard Dreyfuss, and Gloria Grahame.

Claire Bloom as Nora in Ibsen's "A Doll's House."

OLD TIMES *(February 28–March 18, 1972)*

Harold Pinter's drama starred Robert Shaw, Rosemary Harris, and Mary Ure.

AMERICAN COLLEGE THEATRE FESTIVAL IV *(April 17–29, 1972)*

This was the first American College Theatre Festival to be held at the Kennedy Center.

RICHARD II *(May 3–27, 1972)*

William Shakespeare's "Richard II," starring Richard Chamberlain, was the first Shakespearean work to be presented in the Eisenhower Theater.

1972–1973 Season

YERMA *(October 9–14, 1972)*

Federico Garcia Lorca's drama was produced by the Nuria Espert Company of Madrid, during its first visit to America.

THE CREATION OF THE WORLD AND OTHER BUSINESS
(October 23–November 11, 1972)

The American premiere of Arthur Miller's comedy starred Zoe Caldwell and George Grizzard.

THE ENCHANTED *(March 6–31, 1973)*

Jean Giraudoux's romantic comedy starred Elizabeth Ashley and Fred Gwynne.

A MIDSUMMER NIGHT'S DREAM
(April 2–21, 1973)

The Royal Shakespeare Company made its Washington premiere in its production of Shakespeare's comedy, directed by Peter Brook.

THE BLACKS *(May 26–June 16, 1973)*

Robert Hooks and the D.C. Black Repertory Company presented a new production of Jean Genet's play.

Lewis J. Stadlen and Henry Fonda in Saroyan's "The Time of Your Life."

1973–1974 *Season*

MACBETH *(September 17–29, 1973)*

William Shakespeare's "Macbeth" starred Fritz Weaver and Rosemary Murphy as part of the festival, Shakespeare: Dance and Drama.

FULL CIRCLE *(October 5–27, 1973)*

Erich Maria Remarque's drama starred Bibi Andersson and Leonard Nimoy.

A MOON FOR THE MISBEGOTTEN
(December 5–22, 1973)

Eugene O'Neill's play starred Jason Robards, Jr. and Colleen Dewhurst.

JUMPERS *(February 18–April 13, 1974)*

The American premiere of Tom Stoppard's play starred Brian Bedford and Jill Clayburgh.

DESIRE UNDER THE ELMS
(July 29–August 24, 1974)

Eugene O'Neill's drama starred Eva Marie Saint.

1974–1975 *Season*

ABSURD PERSON SINGULAR
(September 4–28, 1974)

Alan Ayckbourn's play starred Richard Kiley, Geraldine Page, and Sandy Dennis.

SHERLOCK HOLMES
(October 4–November 2, 1974)

The Royal Shakespeare Company's production by Arthur Conan Doyle and William Gillette starred John Wood.

THE MEMBER OF THE WEDDING
(January 14–February 8, 1975)

New Phoenix Repertory production of Carson McCullers's drama.

THE MISANTHROPE
(February 11–March 8, 1975)

Molière's drama, produced by the National Theatre of Great Britain, starred Diana Rigg and Alec McCowen.

Giraudoux's comedy "The Enchanted" with Stephen McHattie, Elizabeth Ashley, and Joe Ponazecki.

143

James Earl Jones and Carol Lynley in Steinbeck's play "Of Mice and Men."

OF MICE AND MEN
(March 11–April 5, 1975)

John Steinbeck's play starred James Earl Jones, Kenvin Conway, and Carol Lynley.

THE SKIN OF OUR TEETH
(July 7–August 2, 1975)

Thornton Wilder's play starred Alfred Drake, Martha Scott, and Elizabeth Ashley, and premiered the American Bicentennial Theatre Season of classic and new American plays.

1975–1976 Season

SUMMER BRAVE
(September 3–October 4, 1975)

William Inge's play, starring Alexis Smith and Ernest Thompson, was part of the American Bicentennial Theatre Season.

SWEET BIRD OF YOUTH
(October 7–November 8, 1975)

Tennessee Williams's play starred Irene Worth and Christopher Walken (American Bicentennial Theatre Season).

THE ROYAL FAMILY
(November 11–December 13, 1975)

Written by George S. Kaufman and Edna Ferber, the play starred Eva Le Gallienne, Rosemary Harris, and George Grizzard (American Bicentennial Theatre Season).

LONG DAY'S JOURNEY INTO NIGHT
(December 16–January 24, 1976)

Eugene O'Neill's play starred Jason Robards, Jr., Zoe Caldwell, Michael Moriarty, and Kevin Conway (American Bicentennial Theatre Season).

A TEXAS TRILOGY
(April 22–June 27, 1976,
and August 5–Sept. 12, 1976)

Three plays in repertory by Preston Jones: "Luann Hampton Laverty Oberlander," with Diane Ladd, "The Last Meeting of the Knights of the White Magnolia," and "The Oldest Living Graduate," with Fred Gwynne, played in repertory (American Bicentennial Theatre Season).

1976–1977 Season

THE BELLE OF AMHERST
(September 13–October 9, 1976)

William Luce's play starred Julie Harris.

NO MAN'S LAND
(October 11–November 6, 1976)

The American premiere of Harold Pinter's play starred Sir John Gielgud and Sir Ralph Richardson.

TRAVESTIES *(January 4–February 12, 1977)*

Tom Stoppard's comedy starred John Wood.

ANNIE
(March 1–April 2, 1977)

"Annie" by Thomas Meehan, Charles Strouse, and Martin Charnin starred Dorothy Loudon, Reid Shelton, and Andrea McArdle.

IMAGINATION CELEBRATION
(April 18–24, 1977)

The first National Children's Arts Festival, sponsored by the Kennedy Center Programs for Children and Youth, featured productions of "Jim Thorpe, All-American" and "Light Sings," choreographed by Pat Birch.

THE MASTER BUILDER
(June 1–July 9, 1977)

Henrik Ibsen's drama starred Richard Kiley and Jane Alexander.

DO YOU TURN SOMERSAULTS?
(August 22–September 24, 1977)

Aleksei Arbuzov's play starred Mary Martin and Anthony Quayle.

Sir Ralph Richardson and Sir John Gielgud in the Pinter play "No Man's Land."

1977–1978 Season

A TOUCH OF THE POET
(November 15–December 17, 1977)

Eugene O'Neill's play starred Jason Robards, Jr.

THE FIRST MONDAY IN OCTOBER
(December 28, 1977–February 25, 1978)

The world premiere of the play by Jerome Lawrence and Robert E. Lee starred Henry Fonda and Jane Alexander.

THE MIGHTY GENTS
(March 8–April 9, 1978)

Richard Wesley's melodrama starred Dorian Harewood.

AMERICAN COLLEGE THEATRE FESTIVAL X *(April 10–23, 1978)*

IMAGINATION CELEBRATION
(April 24–29, 1978)

The second National Children's Arts Festival, sponsored by the Kennedy Center Programs for Children and Youth, featured Lukas Foss's "The Celebrated Jumping Frog of Calaveras County," conducted by Sarah Caldwell.

THE LAST OF MRS. CHEYNEY
(August 26–September 30, 1978)

Frederick Lonsdale's play starred Deborah Kerr and Monty Markham.

1978–1979 Season

WINGS
(December 27, 1978–January 20, 1979)

Arthur Kopit's play starred Constance Cummings.

ON GOLDEN POND
(January 25–February 17, 1979)

Ernest Thompson's play starred Tom Aldredge and Frances Sternhagen.

A BEDROOM FARCE
(February 20–March 24, 1979)

Alan Ayckbourn's farce, a National Theatre of Great Britain production.

ST. MARK'S GOSPEL
(March 27–April 1, 1979)

St. Mark's Gospel starred Alec McCowen.

THE GIN GAME *(April 4–May 12, 1979)*

D. L. Coburn's drama starred Hume Cronyn and Jessica Tandy.

COMÉDIE FRANÇAISE
(May 15–27, 1979)

Paris: The Romantic Epoch, a major festival devoted to the music, drama, and art of the French Romantic era. Visiting companies included the Comédie Française, Orchestre de Paris, and Stuttgart Ballet. "La Puce à l'Oreille" by Georges Feydeau, "Le Misanthrope" by Molière, and "Ruy Blas" by Victor Hugo were performed.

HOME AND BEAUTY *(June 1–30, 1979)*

Somerset Maugham's play starred Rosemary Harris and José Ferrer.

DEATHTRAP *(July 24–September 1, 1979)*

Ira Levin's "Deathtrap" starred Brian Bedford.

Ronn Carroll, Tom Aldredge, and Frances Sternhagen in Thompson's "On Golden Pond."

Remak Ramsay starred in "The Winslow Boy" by Rattigan.

1979–1980 Season

NIGHT AND DAY
(October 12–November 17, 1979)

The American premiere of Tom Stoppard's play starred Maggie Smith.

DAISY MAYME
(November 19–December 15, 1979)

George Kelly's play starred Jean Stapleton.

THE ART OF DINING
(December 20, 1979–January 19, 1980)

Presented with the New York Shakespeare Festival, "The Art of Dining" by Tina Howe featured Dianne Wiest.

THE ELEPHANT MAN
(February 26–April 5, 1980)

Written by Bernard Pomerance, the drama starred Philip Anglim and Penny Fuller.

UNIMA 1980 WORLD PUPPETRY
FESTIVAL *(June 9–14, 1980)*

Featured puppeteers from around the world.

CHARLIE AND ALGERNON
(July 31–August 31, 1980)

Music by Charles Strouse, book and lyrics by David Rogers, starring P. J. Benjamin (Kennedy Center-Folger Theatre Group Production).

1980–1981 *Season*

LUNCH HOUR
(September 30–November 1, 1980)

Jean Kerr's comedy starred Gilda Radner and Sam Waterston.

MIXED COUPLES
(November 20–December 20, 1980)

James Prideaux's play starred Julie Harris and Geraldine Page.

PRE-INAUGURAL CONCERT
(January 18, 1981)

The Pre-Inaugural Concert, featuring the Lincoln Center Chamber Music Society, was attended by President-elect Ronald Reagan and Mrs. Reagan.

SARAH IN AMERICA
(February 11–March 14, 1981)

Ruth Wolff's new play, directed by Robert Helpmann, starred Lilli Palmer as Bernhardt. The production was broadcast on public television on "Kennedy Center Tonight!"

THE LITTLE FOXES
(March 19–April 26, 1981)

Lillian Hellman's drama starred Elizabeth Taylor, Maureen Stapleton, Anthony Zerbe, and Tom Aldredge with Dennis Christopher.

THE WINSLOW BOY
(April 29–May 23, 1981)

Terence Rattigan's drama starred Remak Ramsay.

EARLY DAYS *(May 27–June 20, 1981)*

David Storey's drama starred Sir Ralph Richardson.

A TALENT FOR MURDER
(September 1–19, 1981)

Claudette Colbert and Jean-Pierre Aumont starred in the Chodorov-Panama comedy-mystery.

Gilda Radner and Sam Waterston in Kerr's comedy "Lunch Hour."

Coburn's "The Gin Game" starred Hume Cronyn and Jessica Tandy.

CONCERT HALL

1971–1972 Season

NATIONAL SYMPHONY ORCHESTRA
(September 9, 1971)

The National Symphony Orchestra, with conductor Antal Dorati and featured soloist Isaac Stern, opened the Concert Hall.

ISTOMIN, STERN, ROSE TRIO
(September 11, 1971)

Concert inaugurating the Founding Artist Series.

MERLE HAGGARD *(September 14, 1971)*

Founding Artist Concert.

NEW YORK PHILHARMONIC
(September 19, 1971)

First of annual presentations by the Washington Performing Arts Society.

PHILADELPHIA ORCHESTRA
(October 4, 1971)

First of annual visits.

NATIONAL SYMPHONY ORCHESTRA
(November 16, 1971)

Conductor Antal Dorati and featured soloist Ruggiero Ricci.

FISK UNIVERSITY JUBILEE SINGERS
(December 2, 1971)

NATIONAL SYMPHONY ORCHESTRA
(December 21, 1971)

Conductor James DePriest, featuring the Kennedy Center debut of Mstislav Rostropovich.

DUKE ELLINGTON *(December 26, 1971)*

ARTHUR RUBINSTEIN *(January 3, 1972)*

Later recipient of first Kennedy Center Honors in December, 1978.

NATIONAL SYMPHONY ORCHESTRA
(January 18–20, 1972)

Guest conductor Leopold Stokowski.

D.C. YOUTH ORCHESTRA
(March 20, 1972)

First appearance at Kennedy Center.

NATIONAL SYMPHONY ORCHESTRA
(March 28–30, 1972)

Antal Dorati, conductor, featuring the American premiere of Messiaen's "La Transfiguration."

AMERICAN COLLEGE JAZZ FESTIVAL
(May 27–29, 1972)

1972–1973 Season

NATIONAL SYMPHONY ORCHESTRA
(October 10–12, 1972)

Antal Dorati, conductor, featuring the world premieres of Burton's "Fanfare" and La Montaine's "Wilderness Journal," the latter work commissioned by Mrs. Jouett Shouse to dedicate the Filene Organ.

ROD MC KUEN *(November 3–4, 1972)*

ELISABETH SCHWARZKOPF
(December 9, 1972)

Recital.

CHICAGO SYMPHONY ORCHESTRA
(December 10, 1972)

Sir Georg Solti, conductor.

NEW YORK STRING ORCHESTRA
(December 26, 1972)

Conductor Alexander Schneider, Rudolf Serkin, pianist. First of annual appearances during the Center's Christmas Festival.

Antal Dorati, Music Director of the National Symphony from 1971 to 1976.

GUARNERI STRING QUARTET
(February 25, 1973)

   Guarneri String Quartet and Rudolf Serkin, piano.

NANA MOUSKOURI *(March 18, 1973)*

LONDON SYMPHONY ORCHESTRA
(April 13–14, 1973)

   André Previn, conductor.

LINCOLN CENTER CHAMBER MUSIC SOCIETY *(May 19, 1973)*

   First appearance and annually since that date.

INTER-AMERICAN MUSIC FESTIVAL
(May 22, 1973)

   On the occasion of the twenty-fifth anniversary of the signing of the Charter of the Organization of American States, the first annual Inter-American Music Festival held at the Kennedy Center featured Alexander Schneider conducting the Gloria from Casals's "El Pessebre" in place of the ailing Pablo Casals, who made his only appearance at Kennedy Center on this occasion at the conclusion of the concert.

ROBERTA PETERS AND JAN PEERCE
(August 5, 1973)

   Recital.

1973–1974 Season

LENINGRAD SYMPHONY ORCHESTRA
(October 27–29, 1973)

   Conductor Gennady Rozhdestvensky.

ISAAC STERN AND FRIENDS
(November 10, 1973)

STUTTGART CHAMBER ORCHESTRA
(January 13, 1974)

   Karl Munchinger, conductor.

NATIONAL SYMPHONY ORCHESTRA
(January 22–24, 1974)

   Conductor Antal Dorati, featuring the Washington premiere of Penderecki's Dies Irae.

CARLOS MONTOYA *(March 16, 1974)*

John Raitt in "Sing America, Sing!"

DETROIT SYMPHONY ORCHESTRA
(March 17, 1974)

Serge Baudo, conductor.

TONY BENNETT *(April 26–27, 1974)*
Founding Artist Concert.

1974–1975 Season

VIRTUOSI DI ROMA
(October 1, 1974)

NATIONAL SYMPHONY ORCHESTRA
(October 29–31, 1974)

Antal Dorati, conductor, featuring world premiere of Kodaly's "Old Hungarian Soldiers' Tunes."

BERLIN PHILHARMONIC
(November 2–3, 1974)

Herbert von Karajan, conductor.

NEW YORK STRING ORCHESTRA
(December 26, 1974)

Alexander Schneider, conductor.

MSTISLAV ROSTROPOVICH AND
GALINA VISHNEVSKAYA *(March 8, 1975)*
Recital.

LOUIS ARMSTRONG *(May 2, 1975)*

1975–1976 Season

SING AMERICA, SING!
(September 8–21, 1975)

Conceived by Oscar Brand and starring John Raitt in a Bicentennial Musical Celebration of America in Music, Song, and Legend.

HAYDN FESTIVAL
(September 22–27 and 29–30, 1975)

The most extensive festival of performances and musicological meetings devoted to one composer. In all, some fifty concerts were given, including all of Haydn's Masses offered at free performances in the Grand Foyer. The National Symphony Orchestra and the Curtis Institute Orchestra performed many of Haydn's major symphonies; Isaac Stern, Patricia Brooks, and Ilse von Alpenheim were featured soloists.

DIETRICH FISCHER-DIESKAU
(November 1, 1975)

Recital presented by the Washington Performing Arts Society.

A NIGHT IN OLD VIENNA
(December 31, 1975)

Featuring a chamber ensemble under the direction of Alexander Schneider; an annual event since this date as the conclusion of the Kennedy Center Christmas Festival.

KENTUCKY BICENTENNIAL CONCERT
(January 19, 1976)

The first concert in the Bicentennial Parade of American Music featured musicians from every state in the Union during the Bicentennial year.

NATIONAL SYMPHONY ORCHESTRA
(April 6–7, 1976)

Under the direction of Antal Dorati, featuring world premieres of three works by William Schuman: "The Young Dead Soldiers," Symphony No. 10 "American Muse," and "Casey at the Bat."

KENNEDY CENTER SPRING FESTIVAL
(April 18, 1976)

Featuring the orchestra of the Curtis Institute of Music in a series of free concerts of American music.

CONCERT BY MELBA MOORE AND LOU RAWLS *(May 30, 1976)*

COUNT BASIE AND HIS ORCHESTRA
(June 10, 1976)

1976–1977 Season

TEATRO ALLA SCALA *(September 10, 1976)*

Under the direction of Claudio Abbado, the La Scala Chorus and Orchestra performed Verdi's Requiem as part of Teatro alla Scala's exclusive engagement at the Kennedy Center in celebration of the American Bicentennial.

PARIS OPERA CHORUS AND ORCHESTRA *(September 22, 29, 1976)*

Under the direction of Michael Plasson and Seiji Ozawa, the Paris Opera Chorus and Orchestra performed the Berlioz Requiem and also "La Damnation de Faust," featuring soloists Nicolai Gedda, Tom Krause, Jane Berbie, Jean Soumagnas, and Edwige Perfetti.

LEONTYNE PRICE *(October 9, 1976)*

Presented in recital by the Washington Performing Arts Society.

NATIONAL SYMPHONY ORCHESTRA
(October 12–14, 1976)

Under the direction of Antal Dorati, the National Symphony Orchestra featured three world premieres by American composers: Rozsa's "Tripartita," Schuller's "Concerto for Orchestra," and Kay's "Western Paradise."

BALLET NACIONAL DE FESTIVALES DE ESPANA *(November 27, 1976)*

NATHAN MILSTEIN *(December 17, 1976)*

Recital presented by the Washington Performing Arts Society.

The Messiah Sing-Along! in the Concert Hall.

THE MESSIAH SING-ALONG
(*December 22, 1976*)

Annual free Christmas event.

HANDEL FESTIVAL (*January 17, 1977*)

The Handel Festival Orchestra and Chorus performed, under the direction of Stephen Simon, Handel's oratorio, "Saul," for the first Handel Festival, an annual feature. To date the oratorios "Solomon," "Jephtha," "Samson," and "Judas Maccabaeus," and the operas "Rinaldo," "Giulio Cesare," "Semele," "Radamisto," and "Poro" have been performed in concert version.

DAVE BRUBECK (*March 20, 1977*)

PRESERVATION HALL JAZZ BAND
(*March 27, 1977*)

Presented by the Washington Performing Arts Society.

LINCOLN CENTER CHAMBER MUSIC SOCIETY (*April 16, 1977*)

D.C. YOUTH ORCHESTRA (*August 3, 1977*)

1977–1978 *Season*

CLEVELAND ORCHESTRA
(*September 17–18, 20, 22, 24, 1977*)

Under the direction of Lorin Maazel, the Cleveland Orchestra presented the complete Brahms symphonies, the first half of a year-long Brahms/Beethoven Festival.

NATIONAL SYMPHONY ORCHESTRA
(*October 4–6, 1977*)

Under the direction of Maestro Mstislav Rostropovich (his first season as Music Director of the National Symphony Orchestra), Rudolf Serkin, piano soloist, was presented in a program of Weber, Dvořak, and Beethoven.

NATIONAL SYMPHONY ORCHESTRA
(*October 11–12, 14, 1977*)

Leonard Bernstein, guest conductor, and

Mstislav Rostropovich, conductor/cellist. Program devoted to the work of Leonard Bernstein, including three world premieres: "Overture," "Three Meditations for Cello and Orchestra," "An American Songfest."

SHIRLEY VERRETT (*November 19, 1977*)

Recital presented by the Washington Performing Arts Society.

ANDRÉS SEGOVIA (*February 26, 1978*)

Recital presented by the Washington Performing Arts Society.

CINCINNATI ORCHESTRA (*March 19, 1978*)

The Washington Performing Arts Society presented the Cincinnati Orchestra, with Sixten Ehrling, conductor.

URBAN PHILHARMONIC CONCERT
(*May 7, 1978*)

Sponsored by the Kennedy Center Chairman's National Commission to Expand Black Participation in the Performing Arts; Darrold Hunt, conductor.

CONCERTGEBOUW ORCHESTRA OF AMSTERDAM (*May 14–16, 21, 23–24, 1978*)

Under the direction of Bernard Haitink, the Concertgebouw Orchestra performed the complete Beethoven orchestral works.

EVERY GOOD BOY DESERVES FAVOUR
(*August 29–31, 1978*)

"A Play for Actors and Orchestra" by Tom Stoppard and André Previn, featuring John Wood, Eli Wallach, and the Pittsburgh Symphony Orchestra under the direction of André Previn.

1978–1979 *Season*

AWARDS WEEK AT KENNEDY CENTER
(*September 11–17, 1978*)

Kennedy Center-Rockefeller Foundation International Competitions for Excellence in

Daniel Barenboim conducting L'Orchestre de Paris.

the Performance of American Music held its first annual competition for pianists.

FRIEDHEIM AWARDS *(September 17, 1978)*

As part of Awards Week, the Kennedy Center Friedheim Awards' first annual competition for American composition. Five selected compositions in the symphonic field were performed by the Peabody Conservatory Symphony, under the direction of Frederik Prausnitz. The winning composition was "Concerto for English Horn and Orchestra" by Vincent Persichetti.

ANDRÉ WATTS *(October 16, 1978)*

The Washington Performing Arts Society presented André Watts in a first recital of a year-long series devoted to Schubert's piano repertory.

NATIONAL SYMPHONY ORCHESTRA *(November 14–17, 1978)*

Under the direction of Mstislav Rostropovich, the National Symphony Orchestra featured pianist Yvonne Loriod in a concert honoring Olivier Messiaen's seventieth birthday.

NATIONAL SYMPHONY ORCHESTRA *(January 23–25, 1979)*

Under the direction of Mstislav Rostropovich, the National Symphony Orchestra presented the Orchestra's first performance of Britten's "War Requiem" with soloists Galina Vishnevskaya and Peter Pears and with the Choral Arts Society under the direction of Norman Scribner.

JEAN-PIERRE RAMPAL *(February 16, 1979)*

Recital presented by the Washington Performing Arts Society.

PHILADELPHIA ORCHESTRA *(April 9, 1979)*

Conductor Klaus Tennstedt.

ELLA FITZGERALD *(April 15, 1979)*

Recital.

NEW YORK PHILHARMONIC *(April 20–21, 1979)*

Conductor Zubin Mehta, presented by the Washington Performing Arts Society.

LOS ANGELES PHILHARMONIC
(May 6, 1979)

Conductor Carlo Maria Giulini, presented by the Washington Performing Arts Society.

L'ORCHESTRE DE PARIS AND CHORUS
(May 15–18, 1979)

Under the direction of Daniel Barenboim in the opening concert in a series devoted to Hector Berlioz as part of the Center's Festival, Paris: The Romantic Epoch. Featured works were "La Damnation de Faust," "Tristia," "Symphonie Fantastique," "Romeo et Juliette," and the Requiem.

EVERY GOOD BOY DESERVES FAVOUR
(August 7–19, 1979)

Return engagement of Tom Stoppard's and André Previn's "A Play for Actors and Orchestra," featuring Eli Wallach and René Auberjonois.

1979–1980 Season

THE VIENNA PHILHARMONIC
(October 26, 29, November 5, 1979)

Under the direction of Maestro Karl Böhm, the Vienna Philharmonic offered the first of a series of concerts featuring the music of Schubert, Wagner, and Beethoven, as part of the Vienna State Opera's historic first appearance in the United States.

DRESDEN STAATSKAPELLE ORCHESTRA *(October 26, 1979)*

The Washington Performing Arts Society presented the Dresden Staatskapelle Orchestra, under the direction of Herbert Blomstedt, immediately following the first concert by the Vienna Philharmonic.

PRESERVATION HALL JAZZ BAND
(November 11, 1979)

Presented by the Washington Performing Arts Society.

BULGARIAN YOUTH ORCHESTRA and the D.C. YOUTH ORCHESTRA
(December 3, 1979)

Joint free concert featuring the two orchestras, under the sponsorship of the National Park Service.

SING-OUT FOR THE AMERICAN HOSTAGES *(December 29, 1979)*

Sponsored by the Friends of the Kennedy Center and featuring the U.S. Service Bands.

LUCIANO PAVAROTTI *(January 20, 1980)*

The Washington Performing Arts Society presented Pavarotti in recital.

LENA HORNE *(May 12, 1980)*

Recital to benefit the Duke Ellington School for the Arts.

GALA OPENING OF THE INTERNATIONAL PUPPETRY FESTIVAL
(June 8, 1980)

Featuring Jim Henson and the Muppets.

Trustee Abe Fortas, Isaac Stern, and Mrs. Jimmy Carter on the opening night of the Stern Festival.

JOAN ARMATRADING *(July 28, 1980)*
Recital.

ROBERTA FLACK *(August 8–9, 1980)*
Recital.

1980–1981 *Season*

NATIONAL SYMPHONY ORCHESTRA
(September 18, 1980)

Fiftieth Anniversary Concert featuring Galina Vishnevskaya, Isaac Stern, Leonard Bernstein, Jean-Pierre Rampal, and Maestro Mstislav Rostropovich.

CONGRESSIONAL BLACK CAUCUS
(September 26, 1980)

Variety Show.

KENNEDY CENTER-ROCKEFELLER FOUNDATION COMPETITIONS
(September 27–28, 1980)

Kennedy Center-Rockefeller Foundation Competitions for Excellence in the Performance of American Music; violin finals and Friedheim Awards for American Composition.

ISAAC STERN'S SIXTIETH BIRTHDAY CELEBRATION *(October 6–17, 1980)*

Featuring Stern as soloist with the National Symphony Orchestra, under the direction of Eugene Ormandy, Mstislav Rostropovich, Zubin Mehta, Julius Rudel, and Leonard Slatkin.

AARON COPLAND'S EIGHTIETH BIRTHDAY CONCERT *(November 14, 1980)*

Featuring Leonard Bernstein, Mstislav Rostropovich, and Aaron Copland conducting the National Symphony Orchestra in an all-Copland program. The concert inaugurated the "Kennedy Center Tonight!" public television broadcasts.

THE ACADEMY OF ST. MARTIN-IN-THE-FIELDS ORCHESTRA
(November 16, 1980)

Conductor Iona Brown, presented by the Washington Performing Arts Society.

NATIONAL SYMPHONY ORCHESTRA and the ORATORIO SOCIETY OF WASHINGTON *(January 13–15, 1981)*

Featuring the American premiere of Penderecki's Te Deum.

PRE-INAUGURAL CONCERT
(January 18, 1981)

Pre-Inaugural Concert honoring President-elect Ronald Reagan and Mrs. Reagan, featuring the National Symphony Orchestra with Mstislav Rostropovich, conductor, and Eugene Istomin, pianist.

COMMEMORATING ERNEST BLOCH
(February 22, 1981)

The Baltimore Symphony Chorus and Orchestra, conducted by Sergiu Comissiona, performed a special concert in honor of the composer's hundredth anniversary.

FESTIVAL OF FESTIVALS

Carnegie Hall Festival Concerts, featuring the St. Paul Chamber Orchestra with Pinchas Zukerman, conductor. *(May 29–30, June 3, 6, 1981)*

Lincoln Center's Mostly Mozart Festival, featuring the American premiere of the newly discovered Mozart Symphony in F major, K. 19a *(July 7–11, 1981)*

The Aspen Music Festival, featuring the Aspen Festival Orchestra under George Mester, conductor. *(July 20–25, 1981)*

TERRACE THEATER

1978–1979 *Season*

TERRACE THEATER OPENING
(January 28, 1979)

Grand Kabuki of Japan dedicated the Theater, a Bicentennial gift from the government and people of Japan to the people of the United States.

Terrace Theater Inaugural Week also included "A Tribute to Patrick Hayes," "A Tribute to Japan in Dance (The Saeko Ichinohe Dance Company) and Music" (The Tokyo String Quartet), and "A Tribute to Japanese Composers' Influence on Western Music" (Theatre Chamber Players).

MEDIEVAL TO THE CONTEMPORARY CHAMBER MUSIC FESTIVAL
(March 19–25, 1979)

Featured the Guarneri String Quartet, the Waverly Consort, the Schneider-Laredo-Robinson Trio, the Contemporary Chamber Ensemble, the American Brass Quintet, Sergiu Luca, and the Emerson String Quartet.

IMAGINATION CELEBRATION
(April 1–14, 1979)

Third National Children's Arts Festival, featuring Jacques d'Amboise in "An Encounter

Marcus Thompson, John Clayton, and Alison Deane, winners of the National Black Music Colloquium and Competition, with Roger L. Stevens.

with Dance," "Joy, a Musical Tribute to Duke Ellington" (commissioned by the Kennedy Center), and the Empire Theatre for Youth's Kabuki production of "The Sleeping Beauty."

KOBO ABE: THE LITTLE ELEPHANT IS DEAD *(May 8–12, 1979)*

The first Washington appearance of the Kobo Abe Theatre Company.

SOIRÉE ROMANTIQUE *(May 17–18, 1979)*

Evening of French Romantic poetry as part of the festival, Paris: The Romantic Epoch.

THEATRE IN THE AMERICAS
(June 5–10, 1979)

First Inter-American Theatre Festival included companies from Brazil, Canada, and Chile.

SUMMER OPERA *(July 10–August 19, 1979)*

Summer Opera Season, presented by the Kennedy Center and the Washington Opera, included Dominick Argento's "A Postcard from Morocco," "The Impressario" by Mozart, Carl Maria von Weber's "Abu Hassan," Jacques Offenbach's "Christopher Columbus," and Donizetti's "Il Furioso all'Isola di San Domingo."

1979–1980 *Season*

BRITISH AMERICAN REPERTORY COMPANY IN RESIDENCE
(September 3–30, 1979)

Presented the American premiere of Tom Stoppard's "Dogg's Hamlet, Cahoot's Macbeth."

KENNEDY CENTER-ROCKEFELLER FOUNDATION COMPETITIONS
(September 11–13, 1979)

For Excellence in the Performance of American Music (violin).

*Imagination Celebration 1979 featured
Jacques d'Amboise in "An Encounter with Dance."*

TERRACE THEATER ANNIVERSARY WEEK *(February 4–6, 1980)*

Commemorating the first anniversary of the Terrace Theater, featuring the Saeko Ichinohe Dance Company.

MAGGIE MAGALITA *(April 11–19, 1980)*

Written by Wendy Kesselman, "Maggie Magalita" was commissioned by the Center's Programs for Children and Youth for the 1980 "Imagination Celebration."

AMERICAN COLLEGE THEATRE FESTIVAL XII *(April 21–May 11, 1980)*

BOOGIE WOOGIE LANDSCAPE *(June 19–July 12, 1980)*

Written by Ntozake Shange, the play was presented by the National Black Touring Circuit.

THE ACTING COMPANY
(October 1–20, 1979)

First engagement by The Acting Company under the auspices of Kennedy Center offering "Elizabeth I" by Paul Foster, "Broadway" by George Abbott and Philip Dunning, and "The White Devil" by John Webster.

DEATH AND THE KING'S HORSEMAN
(December 4–23, 1979)

A Goodman Theater production of Wole Soyinka's play.

NATIONAL BLACK MUSIC COLLOQUIUM AND COMPETITION
(January 11–18, 1980)

Sponsored by the Kennedy Center's National Commission to Expand Black Participation in the Performing Arts, with the assistance of the National Music Council.

*Peter Grayer and Stephen D. Newman in
Stoppard's play "Dogg's Hamlet, Cahoot's Macbeth."*

1980–1981 Season

DANCE AMERICA SERIES
(September 26–28, 1980)

The Lar Lubovitch Dance Company premiered the Kennedy Center/Washington Performing Arts Society Dance America Series. Other companies presented included Bill T. Jones and Arnie Zane; James Cunningham's Acme Company; Meridith Monk/The House; Laura Dean Dancers and Musicians; The Dance Exchange; and the Bella Lewitsky Dance Company.

MUSEUM *(October 22–November 16, 1980)*

Tina Howe's "Museum," presented by the Folger Theatre Group.

Norman Matlock and Ben Halley, Jr., in "Death and the King's Horseman" by Wole Soyinka.

Richard Howard (left) and Richard S. Iglewski (right) in Alan Schneider's production of Beckett's "Waiting for Godot," presented by The Acting Company.

PAUL WINTER CONSORT
(November 19, 1980)

In concert for young audiences, presented by the Center's Programs for Children and Youth.

THE WASHINGTON OPERA
(December 10, 1980–January 18, 1981)

The Washington Opera season featuring Handel's "Semele," Rossini's "The Barber of Seville," Johann Strauss's "Wiener Blut," and Argento's "A Postcard from Morocco."

DANCE THEATER OF HARLEM
(February 2–6, 1981)

Presented by the Center's Programs for Children and Youth and the Washington Performing Arts Society in a series of free performances for young audiences as part of the Center's Black History Month Festival.

ASPEN MUSIC FESTIVAL *(July 21–22, 1981)*

Part of the first Festival of Festivals.

AN EVENING WITH AARON COPLAND
(September 9, 1981)

Inaugurating the American Portrait Series of Concerts, one of seven Terrace Concert series offering chamber, voice, instrumental recitals, and a sonata series.

BOARD OF TRUSTEES

PHOTO CREDITS